MUAMMAR
AL-QADDAFI'S

LIBYA

KIMBERLY L. SULLIVAN

 TWENTY-FIRST CENTURY BOOKS | **MINNEAPOLIS**

Consultant: Joshua Messner, editor and Islamic scholar, Luther Seminary,
Saint Paul, Minnesota

Twenty-First Century Books
A division of Lerner Publishing Group, Inc.
241 First Avenue North
Minneapolis, MN 55401 U.S.A.

Website address: www.lernerbooks.com

Library of Congress Cataloging-in-Publication Data

Sullivan, Kimberly L.
    Muammar al-Qaddafi's Libya / by Kimberly L. Sullivan.
      p.   cm. — (Dictatorships)
    Includes bibliographical references and index.
    ISBN 978–0–8225–8666–1 (lib. bdg. : alk. paper)
      1. Libya—Juvenile literature. 2. Qaddafi, Muamma—Juvenile literature.
    I. Title.
    DT215.S85 2009
    961.204'2—dc22   2008000405

Manufactured in the United States of America
1 2 3 4 5 6 – DP – 14 13 12 11 10 09

CONTENTS

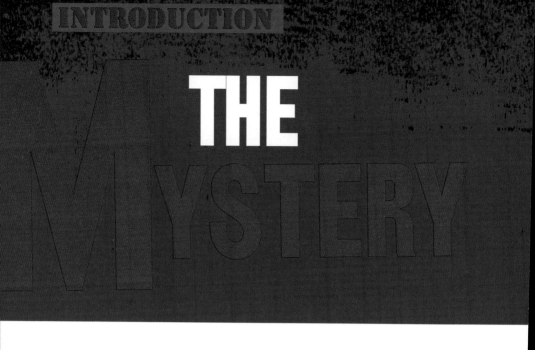

THE
MYSTERY

AT TWO O'CLOCK IN THE MORNING OF APRIL 15, 1986, U.S. Navy and Air Force planes dropped bombs on multiple targets in the Libyan cities of Tripoli and Benghazi. The bombing was ordered by U.S. president Ronald Reagan. It was in retaliation for Libya's involvement in the terrorist bombing of a disco in West Berlin, Germany, on April 5, which had killed two U.S. soldiers and wounded more than fifty other people.

One of the areas the U.S. planes targeted was the al-Aziziya Barracks. U.S. agents believed Libyan leader Colonel Muammar al-Qaddafi and his family were staying there. Colonel Qaddafi was not injured in the attack, although about 130 others were killed and many more wounded. Among the dead was a little girl named Hanna. Qaddafi said she was his adopted daughter.

Like so many aspects of Qaddafi's reign in Libya, Hanna's death

A CHILD WALKS THROUGH THE WRECKAGE LEFT AFTER U.S. PLANES BOMBED Tripoli, Libya, in 1986. The attack targeted Muammar al-Qaddafi and his family, who were staying in army housing there.

was not a straightforward story, however. While Qaddafi alleged that the deceased girl was part of his family, there is a report that this was not the case. Journalist Barbara Slavin was in Tripoli at the time of the bombing. She saw the body of a little girl that had been buried in the rubble of a house. The house was in an upscale neighborhood near the French Embassy.

When Qaddafi later said that his adopted daughter was among the dead, Slavin believed he meant the little girl whose home had been in the French Embassy neighborhood. However, this is not where Qaddafi's family was sleeping the night of the bombing. The contradiction suggests that Qaddafi might have claimed the girl as his own only after she was dead.

Furthermore, accounts differ as to the girl's age. According to Slavin, the child was about eighteen months old, while a *New York Times* article puts Hanna's age at four years old. In a third source, the child was an infant.

The truth behind the story, including the girl's age and whether she was actually Qaddafi's daughter, has been a matter of debate ever since the attack decades ago. But being in the center of controversy is nothing new for Libya and its eccentric leader, Colonel Muammar al-Qaddafi.

Since 1969, when Qaddafi overthrew the old monarchy in Libya, his regime has been accused of everything from state-sponsored terrorism to creating weapons of mass destruction to human rights violations. Despite this, in 2004 the United States reopened diplomatic relations with the country after many years of tension. Under the circumstances, it is perhaps no surprise that confusion surrounds something as straightforward as whether or not Libya's leader had an adopted daughter.

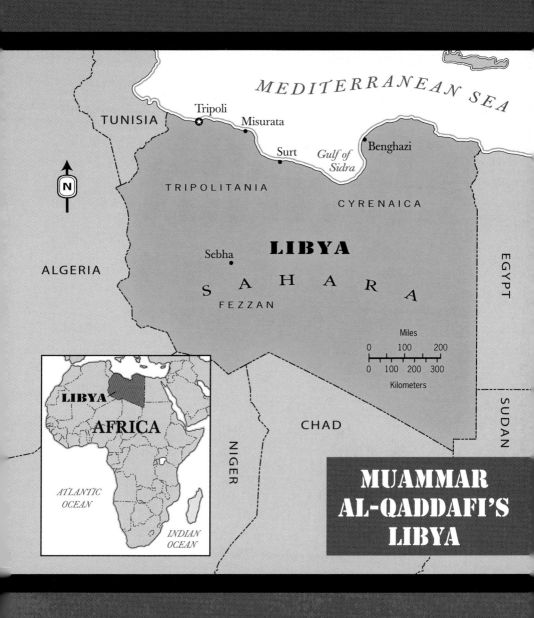

MEDITERRANEAN SEA

TUNISIA

Tripoli
Misurata

Surt   *Gulf of Sidra*   Benghazi

TRIPOLITANIA

CYRENAICA

N

LIBYA

Sebha

S A H A R A

ALGERIA

FEZZAN

EGYPT

Miles
0   100   200
0   100   200   300
Kilometers

LIBYA

AFRICA

ATLANTIC
OCEAN

INDIAN
OCEAN

NIGER

CHAD

SUDAN

MUAMMAR
AL-QADDAFI'S
LIBYA

BEGINNINGS

LIBYA IS A YOUNG COUNTRY WITH AN ANCIENT HISTORY. For thousands of years, nomads have herded their animals across the Sahara in search of food and water. Conquerors from the Greeks and Romans to the Ottoman Turks and modern Italians have long been lured by the ports that dot Libya's northern coast along the Mediterranean Sea. Traders have led caravans of camels through the Sahara to bring valuable goods from southern Africa to people living along the Mediterranean. Despite this the modern nation of Libya has only existed since 1951, when the United Nations granted it independence from Italy. The discovery of oil in Libya in 1959 gave the new nation a promising future.

Colonel Muammar al-Qaddafi led the group of military officers who took over the nation in 1969. He was only twenty-seven years old. A youthful country had a youthful leader.

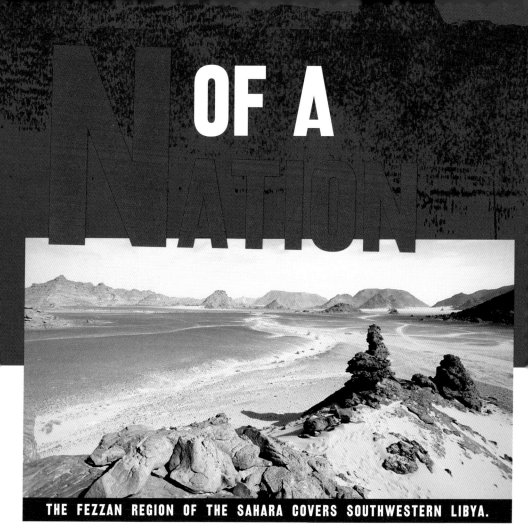

OF A NATION

THE FEZZAN REGION OF THE SAHARA COVERS SOUTHWESTERN LIBYA.
The region consists mostly of barren gravel plains.

GEOGRAPHY AND HISTORY

The Sahara is a desert that makes up about 90 percent of Libya's landmass, yet it is such an unfriendly environment that few can survive there. Many people living in the desert can be found near oases. The springs at oases provide water to raise animals and crops.

The vast majority of Libya's nearly six million citizens live along the Mediterranean Sea, on the country's northernmost land. Much of this area receives enough rainfall to allow for some farming, although the climate in all of Libya is generally hot and dry. Libya's largest cities, Tripoli (the capital) and Benghazi, are located on the coast.

Most of the population of Libya is a mix of Arabs and Berbers. The Berbers are descended from the original people who have lived in Libya for thousands of years. *Berber* comes from the Latin meaning "barbarian," and it is still used by some to refer to the non-Arabs in North Africa. Berbers call themselves Imazighan, or "free people." Bedouins—desert nomads—arrived from the Arabian Peninsula in the 1000s.

Modern Libya only emerged in its current form after World War II (1939–1945). Before that the land that forms Libya was made up

A BERBER MAN WATCHES HIS CAMEL HERD DURING A BREAK IN HIS journey across the desert. Some Berbers hold to the nomadic herding life traditional to their people, but many have moved to Libyan cities to work.

SAHARA

This desert covers one-third of North Africa and makes up close to 90 percent of Libya's land area. It is a harsh environment largely covered in sand—including some massive sand dunes—and rocky ground. Scattered throughout this desert are oases, areas where water comes from underground springs. In these areas, plants can grow and sometimes entire villages can survive. Water is crucial in the desert since daytime temperatures sometimes soar to over 130°F (56°C). At night temperatures below freezing are common.

of three regions: Cyrenaica, Tripolitania, and Fezzan. These regions were ruled by a long list of conquerors who came and went over the centuries. The invaders included the Greeks more than two thousand years ago. Romans followed them, and Arabs arrived in the seventh century A.D. The Arabs brought Islam and the Arabic language, both of which were adopted by many people who lived in the regions presently called Libya. Islam follows the teachings of the Quran, the Muslim holy book, and of the prophet Muhammad in worshipping Allah (God). Approximately 98 percent of modern Libyan citizens are Muslims, and Arabic is the country's official language.

The Ottoman Empire, also known as the Turkish Empire, conquered most of the three regions in the 1600s. In 1911 Italy defeated the Ottomans in Africa and took control of Cyrenaica, Tripolitania, and Fezzan. In 1934 Italy joined the three regions into one united colony and named it Libya. *Libya* was a term that the Greeks had used centuries before to describe much of North Africa.

Tripolitania is the westernmost area of the three regions and was closely associated with Libya's neighbors to the west, including Tunisia and Algeria. There is no natural border between Tripolitania and Tunisia, which means that people routinely cross the border. Tripolitania is the home of many descendants of the region's original Berber people. Cyrenaica to the east identified more closely with nearby eastern countries, including Egypt. Again, border crossings between the two are common, and Cyrenaica is home to many Bedouins. Fezzan, in the southwestern part of modern Libya, had ties to tribes that operated trade routes through the desert. These tribes were known for their independent spirit and ability to survive the harsh conditions of their environment.

An example of the lack of national unity in the country was Libya's opposition to Italian colonial rule. The three regions were unable to work together to fight the Italians after Italy invaded in 1911. There was bickering among tribes, and some city dwellers

BEDOUINS

The Bedouin lifestyle is dying out in Libya. The country has seen a steady decrease in the number of Bedouin people living the nomadic life of their ancestors. While Libya is home to approximately six million people, fewer than two hundred thousand of them are Bedouin. Modern Libyans are moving to the cities, where there are jobs, schools, and medical facilities. Providing these services to people in large communities is easier for governments than offering them to a dispersed rural population, so Qaddafi's regime encourages the urban migration.

early twentieth century. The corps fought rebellious Bedouin groups who refused Italian rule in Cyrenaica.

from Tripolitania sought to create their own independent state. The Bedouin people from Libya's desert regions held no nationalistic (patriotic) feelings toward their country. They traveled the desert freely and fought the Italian invaders in defense of Islam and for the freedom they had enjoyed for generations.

WORLD WAR II

Italy's attempts to integrate the regions of Cyrenaica, Tripolitania, and Fezzan into a united Libya barely took hold before World War II nearly drove the regions apart once again. Italy joined Germany

BRITISH TANKS PURSUE THE GERMAN AND ITALIAN ARMIES ACROSS THE
Libyan desert during World War II. In early 1943, Axis forces retreated from the
Egyptian border across northern Libya, abandoning Tripoli at the end of January.

and Japan (the Axis powers) fighting against the Allies—the United
States, Great Britain, France, and most of the rest of Europe. Since
Libya was an Italian colony, it was officially part of the Axis pow-
ers during World War II. However, a large number of Cyrenaicans
showed their resistance to Italian occupation by seeking to aid the
British.

Tripolitanian leaders were less enthusiastic about siding with
the British. They feared Italian punishment if the Allies were to lose.
Muhammad Idris, a Cyrenaican, managed to win enough support
from Cyrenaicans to arrange for an alliance with the British during

an August 1940 meeting in Cairo, Egypt. Thereafter, many Libyans did what they could to support the Allied powers during the war.

Battles raged across Libya, with control of Cyrenaica switching from the Allied to Axis powers more than once. Eventually, the Allies defeated the Axis powers once and for all. Italy was finally driven from Libya.

In 1945 at a conference in Potsdam, Germany, the Allies debated what to do with former enemy-controlled areas after the war. The conference considered several proposals for the Italian colonies. One involved separating Libya into three regions again and putting each region under the protective wing of a different Allied power. Under this proposal, Tripolitania would have been governed by the Soviet Union, Fezzan would have gone to France, and Cyrenaica to Britain.

"If . . . the Four Powers [France, the Soviet Union, United States, and United Kingdom] are unable to agree upon their disposal [of former Italian possessions in Africa] within one year from the coming into force of the Treaty of Peace with Italy, the matter shall be referred to the General Assembly of the United Nations for a recommendation, and the Four Powers agree to accept the recommendation."

—Allied powers peace treaty with Italy, February 1947

This proposal was not acceptable to all sides, however, and the debate continued. Finally, Britain suggested independence for Libya. It took United Nations (UN) involvement to finally make the idea a reality. In November 1949, a UN resolution was passed to create an independent nation. With the uniting of Cyrenaica, Tripolitania, and Fezzan into one state, modern Libya was born.

AN INDEPENDENT LIBYA

A Libyan monarchy was established by the Libyan constitution in October 1951. Muhammad Idris, who had been largely responsible for allying his country with the British during the war, became the first king—Idris I. The country adopted a federal structure, meaning that the central government was powerful, but a good deal of authority was held by local and provincial governments.

In 1951, when Libya finally became independent, it was one of the world's poorest countries. Only a tiny percentage of the land could be used for farming or pas-

MUHAMMAD IDRIS WAS A POLITICAL and religious leader in Cyrenaica before he became king of Libya in 1951.

ture. Its prospects for improvement were dim since 90 percent of its population could not read or write. This left much of the country dependent on economic aid from those nations that had been victorious in World War II.

King Idris welcomed and maintained close relationships with a number of Western nations, including the United States, Britain, and France. His country enjoyed financial assistance from its friends, as well as help in improving agriculture and education. With this assistance, Idris was able to establish the University of Libya in 1955. The United States and Great Britain were granted rights to build military bases in Libya. Many Libyans resented this dependence on Western, non-Islamic nations and their growing influence in Libya.

Then in 1959, the U.S. oil company Esso (which later became ExxonMobil) discovered large petroleum deposits in the Cyrenaica region of Libya. The discovery of Libya's vast oil reserves brought huge sums of money to the country. It was not long before Libya was the fourth-largest oil producer in the world. Its crude oil was of a high quality, which made it even more valuable on the world market. And because of Libya's location on the Mediterranean, it was easier to ship oil from Libya to southern Europe than from many Middle Eastern oil-producing nations.

Thanks to oil production, the Libyan yearly per capita income jumped from about thirty dollars per year in 1951, when the country became independent, to two thousand dollars per year by 1969. King Idris's government had access to many studies and the advice of Western experts about how to build the country's economy. All the data had been provided by European neighbors and the United States during the years when Libya was receiving economic aid from them. By the late 1960s, Libya was poised for serious economic development.

ESSO BUILT THIS OIL STORAGE AND REFINERY FACILITY NEAR THE GULF of Sidra in 1959. It received oil via pipelines from Fezzan and Cyrenaica.

However, that was not happening under King Idris's leadership. The country was certainly changing as a result of the oil revenue. Oil money had gone to improve the education system, so the growing generation was better educated than its parents. Libyans began leaving their traditional agricultural way of life and heading to the cities in search of jobs. The nation that had once been three separate provinces began to adopt a national identity with less friction among those regions.

HOT!

The highest temperature ever recorded on Earth was in al-Azizya, Libya, on September 13, 1922. It reached 136°F (58°C)!

In spite of the large increase in per capita income, too much of the oil money was in reality benefiting too few people. Political scandals reached into the highest levels of government. Resentment was building against the king and his government. Most Libyan citizens considered King Idris's regime corrupt and too strongly allied with Western nations.

CHAPTER 2

RISE OF A

THROUGHOUT THE ITALIAN OCCUPATION OF LIBYA, World War II, and the establishment of an independent state, many Libyans struggled with economic hardships. The family of Libya's future leader was no exception. In 1942 Muammar al-Qaddafi was born in the Sirte Desert, on the eastern border of Tripolitania. He was the youngest child of a poor Bedouin family living a nomadic life. Qaddafi's father was an animal herder. The family lived in a tent, which they could take down and move as they traveled with their herds in search of food and water.

Qaddafi's relatives had fought for many years against Italian colonial rule. Many Libyans had resisted the Italian occupiers in their country, and the Bedouin people were particularly known for their ferocity in defending their freedom. Qaddafi's father even served prison time for his activities against the Italians.

BEDOUIN HERDERS MAKE CAMP AT AN OASIS IN TRIPOLITANIA IN THE 1930S.

Qaddafi comes from a Bedouin family.

During Qaddafi's early years, he benefited from the education system that was beginning to improve following Libya's independence. He attended school in the city of Sabha, in the desert region of Fezzan. His primary school education included training in the Islamic faith.

While he was a young student, Qaddafi learned about Egypt's president Gamal Abdel Nasser. Nasser had been part of the Egyptian revolution in 1952 that had toppled that country's monarchy. Nasser supported the idea of uniting the nations of the Arab world so they could work together to achieve their common goals. One goal was to separate their countries from Western influence and alliances, which were continuing the history of Western colonization and control. This might have seemed like an unrealistic goal to many people, but Qaddafi had grown up in a family that had actively fought the Italian occupying forces. His family's political idealism had clearly left an impression on him. He identified with Nasser, who had also come from humble roots. He began to idolize the Egyptian ruler and dreamed of following in his footsteps.

EGYPT'S LEADER, GAMAL ABDEL Nasser, hoped to create a union of Arab countries in Africa and the Middle East.

While Qaddafi was still in school in Sebha, he began speaking out against King Idris's monarchy, just as Nasser had spoken out against the former Egyptian king. Both were corrupt monarchs who maintained close ties with Europe. Qaddafi was expelled from school in 1961, after he organized protests in the town center and at a local hotel. His father was able to get him into another secondary school

WHAT'S IN A NAME?

The Arabic language uses a different alphabet than the English language. The main way to transliterate words from one alphabet to another is by sound. In English, there are a number of different ways to spell Muammar al-Qaddafi. All of them are equally correct.

Sometimes the name is spelled beginning with the letter *Q*, as in Qaddafi. Sometimes it begins with the letter *G*, as in Gaddafi. Sometimes an al- or el- is added, as in Muammar al-Qaddafi. Sometimes an *H* is included, as in Ghaddafi or Qadhafi. In a website devoted to Qaddafi's speeches and teachings, http://www.algathafi.org/html-english/index.htm, his name is spelled Muammar al-Gathafi.

Colonel Qaddafi is not the only member of his family to have many spellings of his name in English. The first name of his son Saif al-Qaddafi is often spelled "Seif," in addition to the many variations on his family name.

in the large Libyan city of Masurata. Qaddafi continued to speak out against the government while in school there, but he avoided being caught and finished his secondary school education in 1961.

Qaddafi then enrolled in Benghazi's military academy. Some of his revolution-minded friends also attended the academy, and he found new friends there who shared his dissatisfaction with Libya's monarchy. In 1964 Qaddafi organized a secret group of young cadets (students), all of whom wanted to remove the Libyan king. They began plotting the overthrow of King Idris's government. In 1966 the army sent Qaddafi for further military training at the British

Sandhurst academy for training in military communication and organization.

Army Staff College at Sandhurst in Great Britain. He was promoted to lieutenant after the training was completed. When he returned to Libya, he was assigned to a base outside the city of Benghazi.

Qaddafi and his revolutionary friends continued to gather more supporters to their cause from within the army. It was clear to them that the monarchy was out of touch with the people's will. In addition, a great deal of money was flowing into Libya from its sale of oil, and while some Libyans were far better off than they had been, most citizens remained impoverished. They placed much of the blame for the nation's economic problems on King Idris's corrupt, bureaucratic government. People saw that government officials were living comfortably from the oil income, while average Libyans continued to struggle.

In the late 1960s, King Idris's popularity in Libya continued to wane. He was seen as a pro-Western leader, while many of his citizens, particularly younger people, were firmly anti-Western. He was not especially enthusiastic about the idea of Arab unity, one of the major objectives of Nasser's government and of Nasser's followers in Libya. Many Libyans still saw Idris as first and foremost a Cyrenaican, not a man who represented all of Libya.

COUP D'ÉTAT

In light of the lack of support for King Idris, Libya was ripe for a coup d'état, or overthrow of the government. By 1969 a number of groups in the country were preparing to bring about that change. Rumors circulated about a possible military takeover. Qaddafi commented later that "The country was up for grabs in 1969."

The king began to isolate himself more and more from his fellow countrymen. In June 1969, he left Libya to seek medical treatment in Greece. In his absence, he put his nephew and heir, Crown Prince Hasan ar-Rida, in charge.

"The country was up for grabs in 1969."
—Muammar al-Qaddafi, referring to Libya in that year

Qaddafi used this opportunity to carry out his coup. Some of the men under his command requested permission for night training just outside of Tripoli for September 1, 1969. This gave the soldiers an excuse to have armored vehicles near the city. With Idris still out of the country, there was little resistance when Qaddafi and about seventy other soldiers arrived at the palace. After taking the palace, Qaddafi's men went for the police stations and airports. They met no real opposition in either Tripoli or Benghazi.

Qaddafi understood the importance of oil revenues to his country's future. At the time he assumed power, the oil industry in Libya was primarily run by foreign companies. He made sure that the oil-producing mechanisms—including pipelines and ports—were under his men's control.

The next step was getting the message of his revolution to the people. Newspapers were readily available in cities, but 80 percent of the population was still unable to read in 1969, so getting control of the main radio station was important. Qaddafi's men marched into the main radio station, located in the city of Benghazi. The employees weren't eager to lay down their lives to stop the coup members from taking over.

At six o'clock in the morning of September 1, 1969, four hours after the coup began, Muammar al-Qaddafi sent out a radio message to the Libyan people. He said, "In response to your own will, fulfilling your most heartfelt wishes, answering your incessant demands for change and regeneration and your longing to strive towards these ends, listening to your incitement to rebel, your armed forces have undertaken the overthrow of the reactionary and corrupt regime, the stench of which has sickened and horrified us all."

The identity of the coup leaders came as a surprise to observers around the world. It had not been led by senior military personnel.

A YOUNG LEADER FOR A YOUNG NATION

Muammar al-Qaddafi was twenty-seven years old when he and his fellow officers launched their revolutionary coup against the Libyan monarchy. He was younger than the leaders of most other nations' revolutions.

- Libya's Muammar al-Qaddafi: born in 1942, assumed power in 1969. Age: 27 years
- France's Napoléon Bonaparte: born in 1769, assumed power in 1799. Age: 30 years
- Cuba's Fidel Castro: born in 1926, assumed power in 1959. Age: 33 years
- Egypt's Gamal Abdel Nasser: born in 1918, assumed power in 1952. Age: 34 years
- Russia's Vladimir Lenin: born in 1870, assumed power in 1917. Age: 47 years
- China's Mao Zedong: born in 1893, assumed power in 1949. Age: 56 years
- America's George Washington: born in 1732, elected the United States' president in 1789. Age: 57 years

It was headed by young military officers with no connection to Idris's government or to the top military command.

The young Libyan military officers who had worked with Qaddafi to plan and execute the monarchy's overthrow called themselves the Free Unionist Officers Movement. Egypt's President Nasser had used that same name when he led his coup against the Egyptian monarchy years before. Libya's group consisted of military officers, mainly captains, who were generally from poor or middle-class, rural backgrounds. Their families had not been influential in or strongly connected with the previous government.

A few days later, Crown Prince Hasan ar-Rida gave up his claim to the throne. Idris denied rumors that he had been seeking help from Britain to regain his monarchy. The coup leaders assured him that his family was safe in Libya, but he announced his plan to live in Egypt, rather than return home. In this way, bloodshed was avoided.

Once they were in control of the country, Qaddafi and the other Free Unionist Officers set up a Revolutionary Command Council (RCC). The RCC became a twelve-member advisory group to the country's leader. As is the case in many coups, there was some early confusion about who exactly was in charge of the government, but Muammar al-Qaddafi emerged as the leader about a week later. It was announced that he would head the RCC. The other RCC members were identified four months later.

Qaddafi and his Free Unionist Officers were strongly in favor of Arab unity throughout North Africa and the Middle East. They supported the attempts by Nasser to bring about greater cooperation among Arab nations. They opposed U.S. and other Western influences within their country.

QADDAFI SPEAKS TO A CROWD

in 1970, a few months after the coup in Libya.

Despite their strongly held beliefs and political ideologies, the young officers who took over Libya's government had little preparation to lead a nation. Qaddafi was not a polished politician, as his speeches revealed. He spoke plainly, not afraid to offend his enemies or even his friends. He said things that no one else dared to say.

The RCC removed the high-level officials who had led government ministries, or departments, during the monarchy. In just over a year, all the ministries were under the control of members of the RCC. The only exception was Libya's Ministry of Oil, which had to rely on old employees because the RCC lacked the necessary expertise to run it alone.

EGYPTIAN INFLUENCES

Qaddafi used Nasser's leadership in Egypt as a model for his own role in Libya. The Egyptian leader's principles of Arab unity and Socialism as an economic system became major points in Libya's new government. Qaddafi also followed Nasser's lead in opposing foreign—particularly Western—influences on his country.

Following their coups, both Qaddafi and Nasser put the real power of government into the hands of small groups of top officials. Qaddafi elevated himself from the rank of captain to that of colonel when he took over the Libyan government, just as Nasser had done in Egypt. Although Nasser then became president, Qaddafi refused to hold any formal government title. The only title he accepted was "Leader of the Revolution."

Qaddafi also differed from Nasser when it came to the role of

Islam in government. Under Nasser from 1954 to 1970, Egyptian politics were largely secular, which means they were not founded on religion. Qaddafi made a point of including Islam in Libya's political life. He created a role for himself as a spiritual leader of the Sunni branch of Islam, the denomination of Islam to which the majority of Muslims belong.

When Nasser took over in Egypt, he banned all political parties, except one that he called the Arab Socialist Union. When Qaddafi took over Libya, political parties were already illegal under King Idris. Qaddafi legalized one party, also called the Arab Socialist Union.

PRESIDENT NASSER *(FRONT CENTER)* **PRAYS AT A MOSQUE (ISLAMIC HOUSE** of worship) in Cairo, Egypt. Nasser practiced Islam as his personal faith, but he preferred to keep religion and government separate in Egypt.

Qaddafi was eager to work with Nasser toward their common goal of uniting the Arab world, but they would have only a short time to pursue that goal before Nasser died in 1970. Qaddafi took up the cause on his own and attempted to involve other Arab leaders. Egypt's next president, Anwar Sadat, seemed a logical ally. However, Sadat did not have the same commitment to Arab unity as Nasser. He didn't maintain his predecessor's friendly ties to Qaddafi either. This resulted in strained relations between Egypt and Libya. When Nasser died, Qaddafi lost not only a political ally but also a friend.

Other Arab nations were not interested in Qaddafi's push for more cooperation. Some long-established rulers in the Arab world may not have liked the idea of the leader of a successful coup influencing their citizens. Some leaders found Qaddafi too unpredictable to trust.

A NEW POLITICAL IDENTITY

When Qaddafi and his Free Unionist Officers eliminated Libya's monarchy, they sought to model the new government on a form of Socialism. Socialism is a political system that promotes economic equality among all citizens. The government controls production and distribution of goods, so there are no rich or poor. Instead, the ideal is to create a society in which everyone has work that is suited to him or her and everyone receives the necessities of life in return.

The government owns all factories and other means of production in a Socialist society. In a capitalist society, such as in the United States, an individual owning a factory might make a lot of money selling goods produced in the factory. The workers might earn very little for their labor. In a Socialist system, this is considered unfair. In Socialism, all of society shares equally in the profits made by factories owned by the government. If employees of a factory work hard, their factory will be successful and there will be more profits for them to share.

This system is based on theories developed by Karl Marx. Marx was a German born in 1818 who turned the idea of Socialism into an ideology that millions of people embraced. In *The Communist Manifesto*, published in 1848, he and his coauthor Friedrich Engels laid out the foundation for a Socialist revolution.

Following Marx's ideas, Qaddafi's government nationalized—or took from private owners and put under government control—Libya's

SOCIALISM AND CAPITALISM

Capitalism is an economic system based on private ownership of the means of production where workers are rewarded when there are profits. The idea is that people work harder because that allows them to earn more. Workers enjoy the fruits of their individual labor. This is in contrast to Socialism, in which everyone earns what they need, regardless of whether they excel at their jobs or not. If enough people work hard, then the economy will be successful and all of society will benefit. In a Socialist system, the fruits of everyone's combined labor are enjoyed by society as a whole, not by individual workers.

factories, stores, and apartment buildings, so that no one could make unfair profits from the labor of others. Foreign companies that had been operating oil wells and taking oil profits out of the country were expelled. With all of these assets in the government's hands, profits could be shared by all Libyans.

Marx believed that all citizens would be willing to work together toward a common goal of success for the entire society. This is a key assumption in his Socialist theory. However, in practice, this has turned out not to be the case. Instead, people seem reluctant to work hard if they do not get a direct benefit from it for themselves or their families. If they are able to live in the same apartment and get the same allotment for food and clothing whether they work hard on the job or not, few choose hard work.

Qaddafi was interested in encouraging what he called a Popular Revolution. He wanted the Libyan people to be enthusiastic about their state. They were supposed to be eager to work and fight to make the country a truly Socialist society. He also wanted them to encourage the citizens of other Arab nations to adopt a Socialist system. But Qaddafi soon saw that large, powerful, national bureaucracies were not the way to create a revolutionary attitude among his people.

QADDAFI EXPLAINS HIS PLANS for Libya's economy in a speech in the early 1970s.

TAKING CONTROL

Less than four years after seizing control, Qaddafi announced that Libya would undergo another major change. He delivered a speech on April 15, 1973, that formally marked the beginning of his Popular Revolution. The speech, known as the Five-Point Address, described in detail the goals that Qaddafi envisioned for the future of Libya. It called for the following actions:

1) Set aside existing laws and replace them with laws that further the goals of the revolution.

2) Remove from society those who are inferior or mentally ill (i.e., those who do not conform to society's norms).

3) Create a civilian military power to further the country's revolutionary goals and eliminate the wealthy from society.

4) Create committees to keep power in the people's hands and away from those who would abuse it for their own selfish purposes.

5) Cleanse the culture of Libya to eliminate all poisonous ideas from the Western countries.

Not everyone supported these actions. According to Mohamed Eljahmi, a cofounder of the American Libyan Freedom Alliance (an anti-Qaddafi organization), the Five-Point Address "marked the start of Qaddafi's absolute rule." Instead of allowing schoolchildren to take summer vacation in 1973, for instance, Qaddafi forced them to spend the time in class learning about their leader's political ideology. Eljahmi said, "I was an eighth grade student at the time and forced to attend the summer 'cultural school.' We were indoctrinated with revolutionary rhetoric [speeches] and religious teachings."

Qaddafi did not stop with trying to gain support for his ideals from the nation's young people. He imposed harsh penalties on those who spoke out against the government. Anyone who formed a political party could be tried in court and executed. As Eljahmi later noted, this resulted "in public hangings and mutilations of political opponents."

Qaddafi took another idea from Marxist theory and applied it to Libya: the need for revolution. Marx believed that the time would come in society where the workers, or the proletariat as he called them, would grow tired of selling their labor for little money. Marx believed that eventually the proletariat would rise up and claim their country, along with the means of production, for themselves. This was how Marx saw the end of capitalism and the beginning of the Socialist economy. Qaddafi spent decades pushing the need for the Marxist revolution on his people. He said Libya's Socialist system, which focused on citizens, must be spread around the world.

"Let the ruling classes tremble at a Communistic revolution. The proletarians have nothing to lose but their chains. They have a world to win. Workers of all lands, unite!"

—Karl Marx and Friedrich Engels, *The Communist Manifesto*, 1848

Qaddafi laid out the political philosophy that was the basis of his government in *The Green Book*. This three-volume work explained his views on a variety of topics. The first volume was published in 1973 and is called *The Solution of the Problem of Democracy*. It explains the unfairness of a representative democratic system as it is practiced in the modern world. He insists that direct democracy is far preferable, but not as it is normally practiced today. Instead, he offers ideas for a fairer system of direct participation through local committees that directly participate in government.

The second volume of Qaddafi's political philosophy is called *The Solution of the Economic Problem: Socialism.* Here he points out the flaws in a capitalist economic system. He goes on to describe his own unique vision for the Socialist system that he sought to establish in Libya.

The third and final volume is called *The Social Basis of the Third Universal Theory.* It addresses a number of topics, including Qaddafi's views on education, religion, and the place of women in society.

AFTER QADDAFI PUBLISHED HIS philosophy in *The Green Book*, scholars translated it into other languages. Qaddafi hoped other countries would follow his plan.

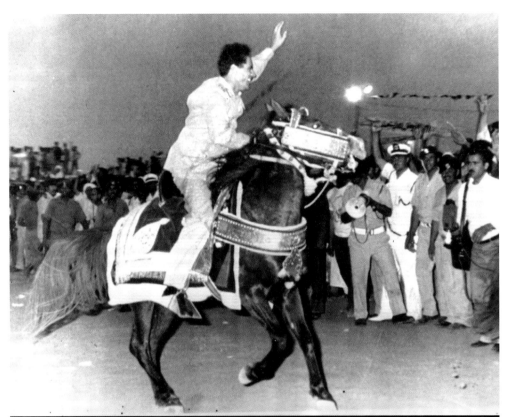

QADDAFI RIDES A HORSE AND WAVES TO A CROWD DURING A 1976 PARADE
celebrating Libya's independence.

NATIONALISM

In addition to his focus on Socialism, Qaddafi has long emphasized another political ideology called nationalism. Nationalism is the idea that people who share a close common political or cultural bond should form a state, or government, with one another. This creates what is known as a nation-state. Cyrenaica, Tripolitania, and Fezzan were only formally united as one nation under Italian

> *"Nations whose nationalism is destroyed are subject to ruin."*
>
> —Muammar al-Qaddafi, *The Social Basis of the Third Universal Theory*, 1978

rule in 1934. Under King Idris's monarchy in the 1950s, they were still largely separate regions. In 1969, when Qaddafi took control, he sought to bring a greater sense of shared identity to his people and the country. By forming a nation, people can work together to promote the interests they hold in common. Nationalism breeds patriotism in citizens of nation-states. Where patriotism exists, people support and defend the nation-state to which they belong.

For many years after the revolution, one of Qaddafi's chief goals was to unite the Arab world. He believed that all Arabs were really part of one nation with one language, Arabic, and one religion, Islam. Qaddafi did not necessarily believe that all the Arab countries should drop their borders and create one nation-state. Instead, he thought they should work as a unified force to attain similar goals. Ideally, unity and a shared purpose among Arab countries could lead to greater success and prosperity for them all.

Despite Qaddafi's strong support for Arab nationalism, other Arab countries made little effort to help achieve his goal. They distrusted Qaddafi and his revolutionary ideas. The result was that he failed to bring together other Arab countries.

FAMILY MAN

Muammar al-Qaddaffi portrays himself as a devoted family man, and he is the father of seven sons and one daughter. He married Fathiha, a member of an old Libyan family, in 1968 and they had one son. That son, Muhamad, is head of the Libyan Olympic committee and runs telecommunications in the country.

He met his second wife, Safia (below), in 1969. She was a nurse who cared for him when he had an appendectomy. They have seven children.

Qaddafi's son Saif al-Islam is a painter and runs a charity. He also has been his father's spokesman internationally in recent years.

Qaddafi's son Saade, a soccer player, runs the Libyan Football (soccer) Federation. He is involved in the Libyan oil and film industries.

Qaddafi's son Mustasim-Billah fled to Egypt after he backed an unsuccessful coup against his father. He was forgiven and returned home to become national security adviser.

Qaddafi's son Hannibal is known to be an international troublemaker. He was once charged with beating his girlfriend and in 2004 was involved in a police chase in Paris, France.

Aisha, Qaddafi's only daughter, is a well-known lawyer.

Qaddafi's two youngest sons are Saif al-Arab and Kahmis.

HOLDING

THE GREEN BOOK **FORMED THE FOUNDATION** for Qaddafi's political and social ideology and the basis of Libya's government structure for the coming decades. His three-volume set of books supports the idea that the citizens of Libya are the ultimate authority and make all rules and decisions.

To achieve this, Qaddafi created the People's Committees to govern in local areas. All citizens over the age of eighteen can vote for members of their local People's Committees. These committees choose representatives to the national level, the General People's Congress (GPC), and report to them. Traditionally, in monarchies like that of King Idris, government power flows from the top down to the people. Qaddafi organized the government so that power flows from the bottom up, supporting his claims of creating a government that really belongs to its citizens.

POWER

A FATHER AND CHILD HOLD UP a poster of Qaddafi at the General People's Congress in 1986. The congress met in Tripoli.

In keeping with this new structure of government and its emphasis on local citizen power, Qaddafi renamed Libya on March 2, 1977. It became the Socialist People's Libyan Arab Jamahiriya. *Jamahiriya* means "a country belonging solely to its people." The Revolutionary Command Council no longer existed under the new government, although the five members remaining from the original coup continued to serve in top positions. Qaddafi headed the Libyan Army along with another former RCC member, Abu Bakr Younis Jaber.

While Qaddafi claimed that the people of Libya were at the heart of the nation's power, that arrangement often did not translate into practice. The GPC was supposed to be responsible for making laws for the entire country. But vital areas of national concern remained in the hands of Qaddafi and his close circle of advisers. These included everything from foreign policy to the military to the country's oil industry.

In addition, the GPC was set up to appoint a secretariat, a group of the leaders of various government departments. This group of secretaries, called the General People's Committee, is responsible for putting together the agenda for the GPC. The agenda they create outlines the daily operation of the nation. The first group of these powerful secretaries was chosen by Qaddafi and those closest to him rather than by the GPC.

Libya took a further step to reach Qaddafi's Socialist goals for the country. In March 1980, everyone had to trade in their money for a new currency. Rather than returning an equal amount of the new currency, the government gave a set amount of cash to each person, regardless of how much old money they had turned in. The idea

THE MAIN LIBYAN UNIT OF currency is the dinar. Qaddafi ordered these new designs for one dinar bills in the early 1980s.

was to reduce the economic differences among Libyans. Citizens were not pleased to lose the wealth that their families had amassed over the years. It created distrust among the wealthier people toward Qaddafi's government, though it won him friends among the many poorer people.

MODERN GOVERNMENT STRUCTURE

The Libyan government has undergone a number of changes since the 1969 revolution. The basic structure retains many similarities to the government created in the 1970s. The country still has more than two thousand local-level People's Committees. These committees are responsible for overseeing many regional issues, such as education and health care within communities.

Although Qaddafi's *Green Book* called for direct government participation by all citizens, it soon became apparent that his lofty ideal was not practical. With limited education and a general lack of interest in politics among the population, leaving important government matters in their hands would not work. Turning substantial power over to the public also would have undermined the authority of Qaddafi's regime. It is not likely that anyone within the government would have been willing to let that happen.

So although the Libyan government appears to be a democracy, the people's representatives have little real power. Local voters elect members of the local People's Committees, but these committees have no power at the national level. The General People's

LIBYANS LISTEN TO QADDAFI SPEAKING AT THE GENERAL PEOPLE'S CONGRESS
in Surt, Libya, in March 2005. That year Qaddafi emphasized the importance of not supporting foreign extremists and terrorist action.

Congress is officially responsible for governing the country, but issues that are of interest to Qaddafi are handled by him and his top government aides.

A number of other informal organizations hold power in important areas such as national security and the court system. The Jamahiriya Security Organization, Revolutionary Guards, Free Unionist Officers Movement, and the Forum of Companions of Qaddafi are just a few of these behind-the-scenes groups operating within Libya. Qaddafi also surrounds himself with advisers from his extended family.

The Libyan court system under Qaddafi experienced substantial changes when he took over, just as the rest of the country did. Prior to the revolution, there were two types of courts—one for regular civil matters and another for issues that had some basis in religious law, such as family cases. Qaddafi created only one set of courts, based on Sharia, or Islamic law. Sharia is law that was developed from the teachings found in the Quran and on the rulings of later Muslim scholars. Sharia has been in practice for more than one thousand years. In many places, local customs have been incorporated into the laws.

The judicial system in Libya has local courts located throughout the country. The verdict of a local court can be reviewed in the appeals courts, found in Libya's largest cities. The most important cases, including those that are based on the Libyan constitution, can be heard in the Supreme Court, which is located in Tripoli, the Libyan capital.

GOALS FOR A NEW GOVERNMENT

Many of Qaddafi's early acts as leader demonstrated his commitment to establishing an Islamic Arab state. He closed non-Islamic places of worship. Some clothing that was considered immodest by Islamic teachings was outlawed, including blue jeans. Public signs, including street signs, were to be written only in Arabic.

Despite personal conflicts between Qaddafi and Anwar Sadat, Egypt and Libya managed to put aside their differences in the early 1970s. The two countries and Syria agreed to create a new Arab state to be called the Federation of Arab Republics. The merger was to become official on September 1, 1973. The unification never happened, however. During 1972 and early 1973, a number of events soured the relationship between Sadat and Qaddafi.

THE WIDOW OF THE ISRAELI FENCING COACH KILLED AT THE 1972 SUMMER Olympic Games visits the room where terrorists kidnapped her husband.

One problem was Libya's involvement in the murder of eleven members of the Israeli Olympic team during the Summer Olympic Games in 1972 in Munich, West Germany. The weapons used in the attack had been smuggled into Germany by a Libyan diplomat. Although German police killed most of the assailants, three survivors escaped to Libya. Qaddafi praised the actions of the terrorists and refused to turn the three over for trial. Egyptian president Sadat joined most of the world in denouncing Qaddafi's actions.

Then, in early 1973, the Israeli military shot down a Libyan airliner that was in Israeli airspace. Qaddafi was outraged and decided to retaliate by attacking Israel's closest allies. He ordered an Egyptian submarine to torpedo a British civilian cruise ship, the *Queen Elizabeth II*. The ship carried many British

ISRAEL AND PALESTINE

For two thousand years, many Jewish people had dreams of returning to their biblical homeland of Israel. After World War I (1914–1918), land in Palestine, then controlled by the British, was set aside for Jews. The Palestinian Arabs who lived in the area resented the Jewish immigration. This created tensions between the Palestinians and the Jewish settlers. After World War II, when Jewish refugees from Europe poured into Palestine, tensions increased. Israel became a separate country in 1948, and war broke out between Israel and a number of Arab states. Israel won the war, but the Palestine Liberation Organization continued guerrilla warfare against Israel, encouraged and aided by sympathetic Arab countries. Though there have been a number of attempts at bringing peace between the Palestinians and Israelis, the conflict continues.

and U.S. passengers. Killing them would have been a deliberate and bold way to drag Britain and the United States into the conflict between Israel and Libya.

If the United Arab Republic unity agreement had been in place at that time, the submarine would have been Qaddafi's to command. Instead, Egyptian president Sadat was contacted about the order. Sadat refused to consent to Qaddafi's planned attack.

That event effectively ended any plans for Libyan and Egyptian unity. Over the coming years, Qaddafi sought to organize other Arab nations around his unity banner but with little success. His reputation for being a troublemaker might have made him seem like an unappealing partner.

OIL: LIBYA'S LIFELINE

At the time Qaddafi assumed power, the oil industry in Libya was primarily run by foreign companies. A chief complaint against King Idris's monarchy was that corruption in the government led to most of Libya's oil proceeds going to top government officials, including the king himself. Little of the oil wealth was actually benefiting citizens. Qaddafi planned to change all that.

Libya needed to keep the oil flowing, so the country's new leader had promised the Western-owned oil producers that he was not going to make any changes to his country's oil policy. But what Qaddafi said and what he did turned out to be two separate things. Within months of the revolution, he demanded higher oil revenues from the oil producers in his country. When they resisted, he threatened to reduce the amount they could pump. They finally agreed to the revenue hikes.

But four years after the revolution, Qaddafi nationalized the majority ownership of every oil company operating in Libya. Later, when he completely outlawed private ownership of all businesses, the decision included oil wells.

Under Qaddafi the money coming to Libya through the sale of its oil resulted in a much higher quality of life for its citizens. Because of oil proceeds, per capita income jumped from about two thousand dollars per year in 1969 to nearly ten thousand dollars per year by 1979. The Libyan education system improved, and literacy rates increased. A massive water pipeline was begun, paid for with

A BILLBOARD CELEBRATES QADDAFI AS THE HEAD OF THE CONSTRUCTION team on the Great Man-Made River Project.

oil proceeds. Called the Great Man-Made River Project, it runs from a large aquifer (layer of underground water-bearing rocks) under the Sahara to bring plentiful water to the cities of Libya.

Not all of Libya's oil wealth was spent to benefit its citizens. Qaddafi also gave considerable amounts of money to fund terrorist groups around the world, including the Palestine Liberation Organization (PLO) fighting against Israel and even the Irish Republican Army (IRA) fighting British rule in Ireland. In the early 1980s, Libya purchased many weapons from the Soviet Union and France. It bought more equipment than it needed to build up its own armed forces. Many of the weapons were clearly being distributed to terrorist groups around the world.

ISRAEL AND LIBYA

Qaddafi has been a staunch opponent of the State of Israel. He believes that the Jews must be removed from that region and that Arab nations must help the Palestinians claim it as their own. Qaddafi expelled all Jews living in Libya following the 1969 revolution, sending more than thirty thousand Jews into exile. He further demanded that Jewish cemeteries in his country be destroyed. Many Libyans agree with Qaddafi and have held demonstrations *(below)* supporting Palestinian control of Israel.

Qaddafi's position against Jews and support for terrorist organizations such as the PLO is one of the reasons he has been unpopular among Western nations. When he sought to make peace with the United States in the early twenty-first century, he claimed to have softened his position on Jews. According to Raphael Luzon, chairman of Great Britain's Libyan Jewish community, Colonel Qaddafi's change of heart seems insincere. Luzon said, "Despite Qaddafi's recent declaration that Libyan Jews are welcome to come back and visit, Libyan authorities have refused to grant me permission to visit Libya three times."

Qaddafi's critics pointed to his weapons spending as wasteful. They said he had a country full of people who needed the oil money for necessities such as health care and improved infrastructure—housing, roads, and electricity.

The importance of oil revenue to the Libyan economy cannot be overstated. Oil was almost the country's sole export in 1973 and after. Agriculture and manufacturing contributed very little to the economy. In the 1980s, however, Libya's foreign policy and support for terrorism were causing difficulty in trading its oil with other nations.

LOVED AND HATED

Qaddafi's personality has played a role in his success as the Libyan leader for many decades. When he took over the country, he knew what to say to gain popular support. He also identified with Libyan anti-Western feelings and made the most of them.

Particularly in his early years as leader, Qaddafi did not shy away from confrontation. This made him both popular among his people for facing down Western influences and unpopular because those confrontations sometimes harmed his people. His support of international terrorism led to international sanctions that damaged the Libyan economy. Economic sanctions included the refusal by other countries to sell goods to Libya, as well as the refusal to purchase Libyan oil. The United States refused to buy shipments of Libyan crude oil and eventually banned other Libyan oil-related products as well.

By the mid-1980s, Libya had no economic or diplomatic ties

with Western nations, including the United States and Great Britain. Libya became more isolated because the citizens of many countries were not permitted to travel there, and Libya's students were not invited to study abroad.

Remaining in control for four decades in Libya is an impressive feat. As the longtime leader of Libya, Muammar al-Qaddafi is no stranger to political opponents, but he has managed to keep them at bay. He does so partly through his wariness and partly by dealing harshly with anyone caught opposing him. Qaddafi uses the death penalty as a weapon against those who engage in political activities that do not support his regime. This includes those who try to form political parties and even those who have left the country to speak openly about life in Libya. Many Libyan political dissidents (those who speak out against the government) have been killed over the years, as have journalists who were critical of Qaddafi's government.

Qaddafi's position at the head of government has not always been secure. He made enemies early on when he took control within the Revolutionary Command Council. The other members of the RCC had expected they would share in governing the country. Not all the citizens backed Qaddafi, either. Increased government control over their daily lives was not popular, nor was the imposition of Islamic law.

The Libyan leader sought to gain support from his people by demonstrating that the change that had taken place on September 1, 1969, was not just a military coup. It was a revolution that came from the will of the people. He always took pains to point out that the date of his coup was Libya's true Independence Day—not the 1951 date when the UN granted Libya its independence. The nation was finally free of other countries' oversight in 1969.

Qaddafi was also given credit for removing the British and U.S. military bases from Libyan soil. The bases had been permitted by King Idris during the years he encouraged Western influence in Libya. They were evidence of this past influence and had long been a sore point among Libyans. Libyans from all around the country supported Qaddafi's removal of the bases.

Qaddafi never hesitated to make sweeping changes in Libyan society in order to mold the nation to his own personal ideology. These changes were not always favored by everyone living in Libya or within the international community. To clean

QADDAFI SPEAKS TO THOUSANDS OF PEOPLE GATHERED TO CELEBRATE the expulsion of U.S. troops from Libya in 1970.

the country of the evils of Western influences, he expelled Italians. Many of them had lived in Libya since the early days of Italian occupation. He forced the Italians to exhume (dig up) their dead and return them to Italy—and he televised the event. He also took over Christian cathedrals in Tripoli and Benghazi. The Tripoli site became a mosque, and the Benghazi church became headquarters for the government's political party, the Arab Socialist Union.

IN GOOD COMPANY?

Every year *Parade* magazine compiles a list of the world's worst dictators. In 2007 it ranked Libya's Muammar al-Qaddafi number 9. This was up from number 11 in 2006. He shared the list with world leaders such as King Abdullah of Saudi Arabia (5) and Omar al-Bashir of Sudan (1).

According to *Parade*, a dictator is "a head of state who exercises arbitrary authority over the lives of his citizens and who cannot be removed from power through legal means. The worst commit terrible human rights abuses." The magazine also notes that in 2006 both Qaddafi and Pakistan's Pervez Musharraf slipped out of the top ten, where they had both been in 2005. But *Parade* noted that this change was "not because their conduct has improved but because other dictators have gotten worse." By 2007 Qaddafi was back up in the top ten.

OPPOSITION TO QADDAFI

Qaddafi's history of doing whatever he felt was necessary to stay in power goes back to the beginning of his rule in 1969. At that time, just months after the revolution, there was already a plot to overthrow his regime. In fact, a number of plots against Qaddafi's leadership were uncovered in the early years of his rule. Hundreds of members of the Libyan military police force were arrested for their involvement in organizing coup attempts. No one came close to success in eliminating Qaddafi, however. The plots just made him more careful and alert to such plans.

The first serious coup attempt against Qaddafi came in 1975. The dispute was largely based on political ideology, in particular how Libya's oil money should be spent. On one side of the dispute were those who wanted the government to make and follow an organized plan to build the Libyan economy. On the other side were those who, like Qaddafi, believed Libya should push its goals of Arab unity and revolution and spend its money on those pursuits.

The coup was led by two of Qaddafi's original RCC members. Their plans failed, and they were caught. By then the original RCC was reduced to only five members, including Qaddafi. In the wake of the failed coup, he took the opportunity to further consolidate his power by removing any government officials who spoke out against his policies. It was not long before many high-level positions in the military and government were filled with those who had family connections and loyalty to Qaddafi.

Even Libyans living outside of the country were not free to criticize the Qaddafi government. In 1980 he ordered government

agents to hunt down these dissidents, whom he called "stray dogs."
Many people became the victims of these Libyan agents. Libyan citizen Faisal Zagallai was almost one of these victims. He was attending college in the United States when an assassin failed in an attempt to kill him.

Through Qaddafi's personal charisma, popular policies, and tight grip on the reins of government, Libyan citizens did not mount any other serious opposition to his rule until the late 1980s. During the first twenty years of Qaddafi's reign, many Libyans were more concerned with their own lives than with national politics. Even in 1986, when the United States apparently targeted Colonel Qaddafi during bombing raids in the Libyan cities of Tripoli and Benghazi, the country's masses showed little outrage.

When oil prices dropped in the late 1980s, Libya experienced an economic crisis. As Libyan citizens felt the economic pinch, their interest in politics began to increase. Libya's generous spending on the military and its disputes with foreign governments over the nation's support of terrorist groups began to drag down Qaddafi's administration.

As the country entered the 1990s, it became clear that change was needed. No longer could Qaddafi run Libya any way he pleased. There was growing opposition to him, both in and out of his country. An organization called the National Front for the Salvation of Libya had been formed in 1981. This group opposes Qaddafi and seeks to overthrow his government and bring Libya a more democratic system. Its members primarily work outside of the country to achieve their goals. The group has joined forces with other Qaddafi opposition groups around the world.

In addition, militant fundamentalist Muslims have been at work in the country. These people are willing to use violent means to force countries to adopt a fundamentalist (strict) form of Islamic government rule.

International sanctions had also put Qaddafi's national economy at risk. First, the United States and then the United Nations stopped importing Libyan oil and products made with it. Other sanctions followed, including restrictions on international travelers to Libya and a ban on arms sales to the country. The international community would have little to do with Libya. If Qaddafi continued to follow this course, it was entirely possible that he would not remain in power long enough to see the new millennium. It was time for him to make some changes.

LIFE IN

LIFE IN LIBYA IN THE TWENTY-FIRST CENTURY in many ways is superior to life in the country at independence in 1951. Income, education, health care, and the status of women are all vastly improved. Oil revenues have paid for many of these improvements. On the other hand, freedom has been limited under Qaddafi's rule. He has censored the media, banned private business ownership, suppressed dissent, and antagonized much of the world.

CREATING A NATION

Before 1951 the residents of Cyrenaica, Tripolitania, and Fezzan had little in common with one another. Even after the creation of

Libya, divisions among the three regions persisted. When Qaddafi took over, this attitude began to change. He and his Free Unionist Officers were seen as citizens of Libya, not of one particular region. Qaddafi did what he could to encourage that perception. As more people moved from their traditional rural homelands to the cities, more of them saw themselves as Libyans, rather than residents of one specific region of the country.

Modern Libya is home to nearly six million people. The country's birthrate is high, which has resulted in a very young population. About 35 percent of the population is under the age of fifteen—compared to 29 percent worldwide. Many other African nations have young populations. Uganda (at 51 percent) and Chad (at 48 percent) have the highest percentage of children among their people. On the other end of the spectrum, in the United States

LIBYAN SCHOOLCHILDREN IN TRIPOLI EAT LUNCH BEFORE A MUSEUM TOUR.

Libya has a very high percentage of citizens under the age of fifteen.

21 percent of the population is under the age of fifteen, while in Japan only 14 percent of the population are children.

Many of Libya's young people have the chance to find good jobs in the cities. Work opportunities are available in the government, as well as in the oil and natural gas industries. In 1975 only about six out of every ten Libyans lived in urban areas. Thirty years later, approximately nine out of ten Libyans were living in cities. Libya's population is growing quickly. In the near future, there will be greater demand for housing, food, water, and health care.

The officers who formed Qaddafi's Free Officers Movement

were young too. Most, including the RCC, were under thirty years old. Many of them were from poor or middle-class families. At that time, the sons of poor families were particularly attracted to careers as military officers. This was because it was possible in the military to rise in social status and success, a move that was not then possible in other segments of Libyan society.

LEISURE TIME

Qaddafi has long held strict views about which leisure activities are appropriate for Libyans. One of the first actions he took after the revolution was to ban alcohol and nightclubs. The complete ban in Libya means that no one, whether they are Muslim or not, may use alcohol in the country.

Qaddafi's position is strict. While some Muslim countries, such as Saudi Arabia, also have a complete ban against alcohol, other Muslim countries do not. For example, two other North African Muslim nations, Morocco and Tunisia, allow their citizens to consume alcohol. Morocco even has beer- and wine-making industries.

The question of sports in Libyan society is addressed by Qaddafi in *The Green Book*. He is mostly against spectator sports, though desert people still race horses and camels. He believes that everyone should participate and not just watch from the sidelines. He even went so far as to ban soccer for many years. He eventually changed his mind though, and soccer is once again allowed. The reason for this change of heart might have been because his eldest son by his second wife, Safia, enjoys the game. The young man, Saade al-Qaddafi, played for professional Libyan and Italian soccer teams. However, more violent sports, such as boxing, are still illegal in Libya.

As for international sporting competitions, Libya under Qaddafi has a checkered past. Libya was involved in the terrorist murder of eleven members of the Israeli Olympic team at the 1972 Summer Olympics in Munich. Libya chose not to send an Olympic team to the 1976 Summer Olympics because it joined twenty-eight African countries in a boycott that year. Since then Libya has sent teams to

SAADE AL-QADDAFI *(CENTER)*, **PLAYING FOR THE LIBYAN NATIONAL TEAM,** defends the ball from Argentine players during a match in Tripoli in 2003. In Africa and Europe the game of soccer is known as football.

a number of the summer games. At the 2004 Summer Olympics in Athens, Greece, Libya competed in judo, tae kwon do, swimming, weight lifting, and both men's and women's track events, though they won no medals. In 2014, Libya will host the African Cup of Nations soccer championship.

WOMEN

Muammar al-Qaddafi's regime in Libya has been a time of greater independence for women. In some Muslim countries, women struggle to have the same rights that women in other countries have. In Libya women have the right to vote, they may hold jobs, and they even serve in the military. Schools and universities offer education to females. Qaddafi's only daughter, Aisha, is a practicing lawyer. Qaddafi even has a group of women who serve as his personal bodyguards. These women, known as the Amazonian Guard, are highly trained in martial arts.

Polygamy (having multiple wives) is not common in Libya, though in certain times and places in Islamic

AISHA AL-QADDAFI SPEAKS BEFORE a concert at the 2006 Hanna Festival for Freedom and Peace, named for the girl killed in the 1986 U.S. bombing raid.

history it has been permitted. Girls under sixteen cannot be forced into marriage, and women may even marry against their families' wishes if they choose. This does not happen often, however. Libyan society is centered on the family, and opposing one's family in this way would be a bold and lonely step.

Libyan law also does not require women to wear the traditional Islamic head scarf in public. Some women—often young and urban—exercise this freedom by appearing in public without a head scarf, but most women still cover their heads.

Qaddafi has made an attempt to free women from traditional roles and restrictions in Libya, but changing his country's culture has been an uphill battle. While females have access to education, their literacy level is still only 63 percent, compared to 88 percent

MUSLIM STUDENTS, WEARING HEAD SCARVES, WALK TO CLASSES AT
Garyounis University in Benghazi, Libya. Women are not required by law to wear head scarves, but many choose to do so for religious reasons.

THE GREEN BOOK ON WOMEN

The views expressed about women in Qaddafi's *Green Book* are an interesting mix of traditional and progressive. Qaddafi says that women are equal to men in many ways and must be treated respectfully: "There is no difference between man and woman in all that concerns humanity. None of them can marry the other against his or her will, or divorce without a just trial. . . . The woman is the owner of the house."

Still, he is opposed to mothers working outside of the home. He believes that it is "harsh materialistic circumstances" that force mothers to leave their children and put them in child care facilities so they can work. He says, "To separate children from their mothers and to cram them into nurseries is a process by which they are transformed into something very close to chicks, for nurseries are similar to poultry farms in which chicks are crammed after they are hatched."

for males. It appears that younger women are making significant educational strides, however, because by 2006, more women had graduated from Libya's universities than men.

While Libyan women have greater freedom than in some of the other Arab nations, their status is still not equal to men. Qaddafi's progressive notions about women have met a great deal of resistance in society. This suggests that his views are not shared by all Libyans. Women who work outside their homes generally serve in traditionally female occupations, such as teaching and nursing.

Despite their freedom to work in the fields of their choice, many Libyan women still choose not to enter the workforce. Libyan women average about 3.5 children each. This fertility rate is high by the standards of countries where women enjoy greater equality with men. The rate in the United States is about 2 children per woman. In the European Union countries, it is 1.5 children per woman. A woman still gains status in Libyan society by producing a son.

EDUCATION

Before the 1969 coup, the literacy rate in Libya was approximately 20 percent. This means that only one out of every five Libyans could

BOYS WAIT FOR THEIR TEACHER TO LOOK AT THE VERSES THEY HAVE copied from the Quran. Copying helps them to memorize the verses as well as learn to write. Libyan schools teach Islamic studies at all levels of the curriculum.

read or write. By 2004 Libya reported that its overall literacy rates had climbed to over 82 percent. This change was largely due to improvements in the education system under Qaddafi.

A free education—from primary school to college—is open to all Libyans. Primary schools are widely available in both cities and rural areas. Everyone must attend school until they are at least fifteen years old. After that, if people choose to continue their education, it is free at the nation's colleges. The income Libya received from selling its oil gave the country the opportunity to create a solid educational system for its people.

During Qaddafi's early campaign against influences from Western nations, he ordered that Arabic be his country's official language. Libyan schools taught in Arabic and did not offer multilingual education. The country was largely isolated from the

"Knowledge is a natural right of every human being which nobody has the right to deprive him of under any pretext. . . . Ignorance will come to an end when everything is presented as it actually is and when knowledge about everything is available to each person in the manner that suits him."

—Muammar al-Qaddafi, *The Green Book: The Social Basis of the Third Universal Theory*, 1978

Western world at the time, and Libyans were banned from studying abroad in Western nations. Libya had little tourism, so the lack of signs in English or other Western languages wasn't a problem.

SOCIAL SERVICES

Besides funding education, oil money has provided many other services to the Libyan people. Qaddafi's *Green Book* established the basis for a Socialist society in Libya. The Socialist system demands a wide array of public services that must be provided to a nation's people. Libya offers workers' compensation for work-related injuries, retirement benefits, and survivors' pensions in the case of death. The country also provides food subsidies, employee job protections, income subsidies to the unemployed, maternity leave and child care, orphanages, and old age homes. It is interesting that though *The Green Book* does not approve of mothers leaving their children in child care centers so they can work, the social security system in Libya offers child care and maternity leave for working mothers.

During the 1970s and 1980s, the vast majority of urban Libyans were working in government jobs. This was largely because Qaddafi's government had eliminated most private-sector jobs when it outlawed private ownership of businesses. But changes began to take hold in Libya during the 1990s, and more private businesses were established. Even so, in 2006 more than half of the population was still working for the government, including health care and teaching. Libyans employed in private-sector jobs work in the oil industry and agriculture, among other areas.

HEALTH CARE AND HUMAN DEVELOPMENT

Libya has a national program for health care, and services are free to all residents. This includes treatment at hospitals and clinics around the country and free medications to those who need them. Colleges offer free training in medicine, dentistry, and nursing. The availability of medical care has contributed to an average life expectancy that rivals many Western nations, including the United States. Libyan men live to an average of seventy-four years and women to seventy-eight years.

According to the *Human Development Report* issued by the United Nations Development Programme, Libya's Human Development Index ranking was 58 out of 177 countries included in the analysis. To be in the

THE RED CRESCENT IS THE SYMBOL of the organization for medical assistance in Islamic countries. The Red Crescent partners with Red Cross societies to provide health care.

upper one-third of nations is an accomplishment, especially for a country that was one of the poorest on Earth less than a half century ago. Libya's life expectancy is higher than that of Tunisia and Morocco, due mainly to its improved health-care system. Infant and maternal mortality rates are also lower in Libya than in Tunisia and Morocco, again likely the result of health care that is available to all.

POPULATION DISTRIBUTION

Most of Libya's population lives in urban areas along the coast of the Mediterranean Sea. About 86 percent of Libyans are urban dwellers, which is even higher than the United States' rate of 79 percent. Jobs in the oil and natural gas industries tend to be in cities, and employees move to where the work is. Qaddafi's social and government programs put many Libyans in government jobs, which are generally available in population centers rather than remote areas. Most of Libya's land is desert, where life is hard. The country's oil wealth has improved the standard of living for most Libyans, so that they can leave the harsh rural life behind if they choose.

In addition to Libya's native population, approximately one million non-Libyans live and work in the country. These people, mostly laborers, come from other African countries, including a number of sub-Saharan nations such as Nigeria, Sudan, and Ghana. While the Libyan economy relies on this foreign workforce, these workers' positions are not secure. During an economic downturn in the 1980s, for example, Qaddafi ordered

MEN AND BOYS FROM SUB-SAHARAN NATIONS WAIT BY THE ROADSIDE
in a Libyan town in hopes of being hired to work for the day. In the 1980s, Qaddafi
expelled many thousands of foreign workers when the economy slowed.

hundreds of thousands of them out of the country. Libyans' anger
toward foreign workers in the midst of economic hard times has
sometimes resulted in terrible violence.

MEDIA

SINCE WORLD WAR II, TOTALITARIAN COUNTRIES (those ruled by a dictator) have used a variety of justifications for increasing government control over the media. They have argued that newly formed governments cannot survive internal conflict. The media must support even long-established dictatorships in order to eliminate statements contrary to government policy. Some Arab governments use the Arab-Israeli conflict as an excuse, claiming they need media support while they are at war with Israel.

Qaddafi has claimed that the goals of his regime—Arab unification, a Socialist state that belongs to all, and the defeat of Israel—must be supported by the media. He has also managed to control the media to suppress the spread of ideas that run counter to his programs and beliefs. Many movies and theater performances are banned. The work of Libyan authors is subject

to government censorship. The country's most widely read book is the Quran. *The Green Book* is also popular.

RADIO AND TELEVISION

The Libyan Jamahiriya Broadcast Corporation is responsible for radio broadcasts. It also maintains an Internet news site. Even before Qaddafi rose to power, the government controlled the broadcast service. One of the first things the Revolutionary Command Council did when it seized control was to ensure that the Libyan Broadcast Service took orders directly from them. Furthermore, within hours of the coup on September 1, 1969, Qaddafi took to the radio waves and announced the end of the monarchy and the beginning of a new age in Libya.

Libya has had a national television system in place since 1968, but King Idris's monarchy was not devoted to expanding the reach of television. In contrast, Qaddafi's government needed to have a population that was enthusiastic about the country's direction and willing to work to achieve the nation's objectives. Television became a government priority. By the late 1960s, thousands of Libyans had access to television, and the new regime recognized it as an excellent method for gathering support. The government controls television broadcasting through an organization called the People's Committee of the Great Jamahiriya Television. This committee is overseen by a committee within the Libyan Information Ministry.

Literacy rates in Libya have improved dramatically in recent decades, but at the beginning of the Qaddafi regime, a number of Libyans were still unable to read and write. This meant that the government could not rely on newspapers to get its message to all citizens. Radio and television were vital tools for disseminating details about the government's programs.

Television and radio, like all media in Libya, are closely regulated by the government. A great deal of the programming on Libyan radio and television stations has some form of political message. The Libyan Information Ministry provides a statement that explains the goals of its broadcasts: "To embody the Arab revolutionary objectives of freedom, socialism and unity and to permeate such objectives in the minds of the people; . . . to bind the Arab struggle for liberation of the occupied territories [Palestine] with the cause of liberation and freedom in the Third World."

These goals differ greatly from those of the media in most

Western countries, which emphasize entertainment and corporate profit. Libyan radio stations offer music and news, but Western music is banned. Religious programming is common. Advertising is not allowed during either radio or television broadcasts. Most of the programming broadcast by the Libyan Television Network is produced in other countries. Libyans find much of the small amount of television material generated in Libya to be boring.

Satellite dishes are legal in Libya, and many people have them. Access to satellite television opens up a wide array of additional programming from around the world, much of it far more popular and entertaining than the domestic offerings. One especially popular television network is al-Jazeera.

MERCHANTS SELL SATELLITE DISHES IN THE MARKET OUTSIDE OF TRIPOLI.
Satellite television brings international television programs to Libyans.

In a country like Libya, where media content is tightly controlled, al-Jazeera's uncensored news programming is unique. Al-Jazeera is based in the Arab nation of Qatar, which puts it out of reach of Qaddafi and his government. The network has no obligation to offer stories that treat his regime favorably, so it is

AL-JAZEERA TELEVISION

Founded in 1996, al-Jazeera Television has become an influential source of information throughout the Arab world. Based in Qatar, it received funding from the Qatari government to establish an independent satellite television station. By 2001 a large number of al-Jazeera's staff were from Arab nations other than Qatar. As a result, the Arabic-language station focuses on the entire Arab world. The station's leaders made a decision early on to concentrate on news and current events, even though it might offend one Arab government or another.

Al Jazeera has offered firsthand coverage for many events that Western journalists missed. They were there when the U.S.-led coalition bombed targets in Iraq in Operation Desert Fox in 1998. They accepted the Taliban government's offer to open an office in Afghanistan in 1999, which allowed them to be eyewitnesses to the U.S. invasion of Kabul, Afghanistan, two years later. They even aired an interview with terrorist al-Qaeda figure Osama bin Laden.

not always popular within Qaddafi's government. The only way for Qaddafi to remove al-Jazeera from Libyan homes is to outlaw satellite dishes. But such a move would be very unpopular, so al-Jazeera and other satellite television programs with unregulated content are tolerated in Libya.

In addition to reporting the news, al-Jazeera offers its viewers a number of political opinion programs. The controversial *The Opposite Direction* is particularly popular. This show's host is a Syrian named Faisal al-Qasim. He is known for inviting guests with conflicting views to discuss their differences on the show. He talked to Qaddafi on his program after the September 11, 2001, terrorist attacks in the United States. Qaddafi told him that the United States was correct to seek revenge against the responsible parties.

Success has exacted a price for al-Jazeera Television. Most Arab countries have lodged complaints about specific shows or newscasts that cast their countries in a negative light. Occasionally, countries have gone so far as to close local al-Jazeera offices. Sometimes nations offended by al-Jazeera broadcasts complain to the Qatari government. In response, the government points out that the station is independent. Al-Jazeera itself claims that so many countries get upset by its stories that it must not have any bias. The station manages to irritate everyone equally.

Al-Jazeera's English-language news channel was launched in November 2006. It reaches more than 100 million households worldwide.

NEWSPAPERS

Privately owned newspapers were permitted in Libya under King Idris. When Qaddafi took over in 1969, his government established its own paper, called *al-Thawra* (the Revolution). The publication's primary purpose was to present Qaddafi's views to help gain the people's support for his new government. In 1972 the Libyan government stopped publishing *al-Thawra* and began a new paper called *al-Fajr al-Jadid* (the New Dawn), which continued *al-Thawra*'s work.

Though independent newspapers were still legal after 1969, Qaddafi's regime made it hard for them to compete with the government publications. Only the official paper could carry government-placed advertisements, which brought a great deal of money to the newspapers. It was difficult for Libya's three privately owned daily papers to survive without such an important source of revenue.

Independent newspapers continued to be legal until January 1972, when the Revolutionary Command Council ordered that they stop publishing. This order followed a trial, which resulted in the verdict that the independent press posed a threat to public opinion.

By 1999 Libya had four major daily newspapers, with a total circulation of just over 120,000. Most Libyans are able to read the papers, which are written in Arabic. The content in all the newspapers is strictly controlled by the Libyan government, just as television and radio broadcasts are. No stories can contain negative comments about Qaddafi or about government policies that he supports.

Because none of the newspapers may be critical of the national government or its leaders, the content of all the news-

A TRIPOLI NEWSPAPER STAND OFFERS COPIES OF GOVERNMENT AND independent papers. They all contain positive stories that support Qaddafi's rule.

papers is very similar. By comparison, in the United States and other Western democracies, where there is limited government control over the media, different kinds of stories are published in newspapers or broadcast on television. Some publications or news stations are generally friendlier toward government policies, while others are harsher. In Libya, however, there is no such thing as one paper that is more pro-government than another. All the papers are basically the same. They all offer positive stories about the nation's leadership.

The Libyan media is also used to identify and explain government policies. They assure the people that the new policies are the right choice and that sensible people will agree with them. While most stories are written for the people of Libya, occasionally some articles have an intended audience outside of Libya. These stories usually seek to get a foreign government or group to alter its course, and they will explain the reasons why the position of a foreign power or group is wrong.

CONTROLLING THE NEWS

Most papers are owned by the country's one and only political party. The Arab Socialist Union has been the only legal party in Libya for decades, and it is the party to which all government officials belong. This means that even though the government itself might not technically own the print media outlets, it has complete control over the media's behavior through the party.

In addition to this form of government ownership of the media, controls are placed on the reporters themselves. If journalists in Libya do not abide by their government's restrictions on the stories they print, the consequences can be severe. Journalists who try to print negative comments about the government can be fined or suspended. On the other hand, journalists who cast the regime in the right light might be promoted.

In the past, journalists who have criticized Qaddafi or his regime have been arrested and sent to jail. Some have disappeared completely. The assumption is that the government secretly had them killed or imprisoned.

Although the newspapers in Libya are careful about not criticizing the national government, it is possible for them to say negative things about minor problems at the local level. For example, an article or editorial might complain about poor garbage pickup service. The local officials in charge of the garbage collection might even be mentioned. This allows for the public to have some sort of limited political debate. It does not negatively address issues that are meaningful to the country as a whole.

Newspapers may sometimes report on disagreements that take place in the General People's Congress and the People's Committees. No one is ever allowed to disagree with or criticize Qaddafi himself, however. When foreign newspapers and magazines are imported into Libya, they are censored to eliminate material that might be critical of his regime.

Libya is not the only Arab country that bans criticisms of the national government in the media. Other countries, including Saudi Arabia and Syria, routinely impose such restrictions on their journalists. While Qaddafi's control over his country's media is not unusual in the Arab world, Libya is among the region's strictest enforcers of such restrictions.

One impact of media censorship is that it dramatically limits the level of political debate that can take place in the country. If citizens are not informed about their government's shortcomings, they are less able to debate government actions or the benefits of replacing government officials. Media censorship prevents any serious discussion on points of view that disagree with the current administration within the country.

Libya's censorship promotes support for government leaders by offering positive information about them, and it recruits citizens to accept the government's policies and objectives. Qaddafi needed active support from the people to achieve the ambitious goals of his society. Without their support and approval, it is entirely possible that Qaddafi's regime could have been deposed by a coup, just as the monarchy had been.

STUDENTS CONNECT TO THE INTERNET IN A CYBERCAFE IN LIBYA IN 2000.
Internet use in Libya has increased despite restrictions on certain kinds of sites.

Internet access is growing in Libya. Internet cafés are springing up in cities, though users are not supposed to view sites that contain sexually explicit or political material. Qaddafi's government currently tolerates the growing source of information from the outside world provided by the Internet, even though it is difficult for the government to regulate its content. A ban on Internet access would likely anger too many people.

THE GREEN BOOK

Some people have compared Libya's revolution to the Chinese Revolution when the Chinese Communist Party, led by Mao Zedong, took control of the country in 1949. One similarity between them is that Chairman Mao wrote his views about government and politics in his *Little Red Book*. This book was distributed to citizens in China, as well as to other interested readers outside of the country. Similarly, Qaddafi wrote his three-volume *The Green Book* in the 1970s to lay out his perspectives on politics and government. The colors mentioned in both of the books' titles have important meanings. Red has long been associated with Communism, while green, also the color of Libya's flag, represents Islam.

The first volume of *The Green Book* is called *The Solution of the Problem of Democracy: The Authority of the People*. Published in 1973, it describes the difficulties that are posed by democracy as it is practiced in most of the world. Qaddafi opposes representative democracy, in which citizens vote for candidates to represent them. This is the type of government seen in modern democracies, such as the U.S. Congress and Great Britain's Parliament. Qaddafi points out that such a system results in elected officials who only support the interests of their small districts, regardless of whether or not those interests benefit others in the country. He argues that, in such a system, no one looks out for the good of the nation as a whole.

Qaddafi also dislikes the idea of direct democracy as it is practiced in the modern world. In direct democracy, voters get to make decisions about which actions their government should take. A popular form of direct democracy is the referendum, in which the people are presented with a proposed government policy and then vote on whether or not they support it.

Qaddafi feels that a simple yes or no decision about complicated policy issues does not benefit anyone. He disagrees with any form of democracy that is based on a majority vote. In a majority vote, he points out, it is possible to ignore the views of up to 49 percent of the voters.

IN A TRIPOLI MONUMENT TO QADDAFI'S PHILOSOPHY, *THE GREEN BOOK* STANDS triumphant on top of books of Marxist and democratic theory.

To avoid problems caused by democracy, Qaddafi endorses People's Committees at the local level and a national level Congress elected by the people. The General People's Congress makes laws, which are then carried out by the People's Committees. Qaddafi says this is especially effective because it guarantees that a large number of citizens have the chance to be personally involved in government.

He writes, "Thus, both the administration and the supervision become popular [in the hands of the people] and the outdated definition of democracy—Democracy is the supervision of the government by the people—comes to an end. It will be replaced by the right definition—Democracy is the supervision of the people by people."

This first volume also supports Qaddafi's opposition to more than one political party. He explains, "The party is a dictatorial instrument of governing that enables those with one outlook and a common interest to rule the people as a whole. Compared with the people, the party is a minority."

Part 2 of *The Green Book* is titled *The Solution of the Economic Problem: Socialism* and was published in 1977. The Libyan constitution that was put in place after the 1969 revolution allowed for private ownership of businesses. That changed after Qaddafi published this second book.

The Solution of the Economic Problem outlines the primary goal of Libya's Socialist changes. Qaddafi explains, "The purpose of the new socialist society is to create a society which is happy because it is free. This can be achieved through satisfying the material and spiritual needs of man, and that, in turn, comes about through the liberation of these needs from outside domination and control." To that end, he sought to make sure that Libyans would be free from depending on other people for housing or work. Instead, all things within the society were owned by the state. And since the people made up the state, public ownership meant that everyone owned what they needed to survive.

In keeping with these views, the Libyan government outlawed private business ownership in 1978. The result was not what Qaddafi had envisioned. Production in the country dropped immediately afterward. (Socialism often fails economically under a dictator because a totalitarian regime removes the ability of the people to choose for themselves.) By the late 1980s, private ownership of business was legal again. Since then foreign companies have been encouraged to do business in Libya and invest in new business operations.

Part 3 of *The Green Book* was released in 1978. It is titled *The Social Basis of the Third Universal Theory*. In it Qaddafi spends a great deal of time discussing nationalism. He feels that encouraging unity among the people of his nation is vital. He explains, "Nations whose nationalism is destroyed are subject to ruin. Minorities, which are one of the main political problems in the world, are the outcome of a social cause. They are nations whose nationalism has been destroyed and torn apart."

Qaddafi believes it is of utmost importance that people living within the same country feel connected to one another through a shared background and values. In fact, he places so much emphasis on this notion that he says there should be only one religion in any country to foster closeness among its people.

This volume also addresses other topics, including the roles of men and women in society, as well as education. He insists on the importance of a woman's role in child rearing and criticizes

BOYS LEAN OVER A BANNER that reads, "Yes to the great Libyan people!" Such slogans encourage nationalism in Libya.

educational systems around the world for not allowing students enough freedom to study in the manner that best suits them.

The education section of *The Green Book* suggests that Qaddafi holds little love for the conventional educational system in Libya or in the world. The book notes, "Education, or learning, is not necessarily that methodized curriculum and those classified subjects in text books which youth are forced to learn during specified hours while sitting in rows of desks. This type of education, now prevailing all over the world, is against human freedom." In order to address the education system's problems, he suggests, "All methods of education prevailing in the world should be done away with through a worldwide cultural revolution." He recommends replacing the rigid existing system with one that allows students to learn subjects that interest them and to do so in the manner that best suits their learning styles.

Some of Qaddafi's negative feelings about modern education might have sprung from his own childhood experiences in Libya's schools. He was slapped by one of his teachers while he was a schoolboy, and then he was expelled in 1961 for protesting the government of King Idris.

RELIGIOUS SYMBOLISM

Qaddafi has long used religion to secure his hold on the Libyan people. In order to more effectively use Islam's teachings to retain power, he needed to shift the fundamental religious beliefs of his people. Many Libyans followed the teachings of Sayyid Mohammad bin Ali al-Sanusi. His teachings gave desert dwellers, especially in

جهاز الأعمال العامة

A BILLBOARD SHOWS QADDAFI'S BEDOUIN HERITAGE. THIS EMPHASIZES
that he comes from a modest background and identifies with ordinary people.

Cyrenaica, a form of Islam that unified them in their battles against enemy invaders. The unpopular King Idris I was a grandson of the founder of Sanusi. Qaddafi encouraged his people to reject the Sanusi traditions and adopt Sunni Muslim teachings. He had government agents harass Sanusi followers.

Despite his desire to achieve status as a religious leader in Libya, Qaddafi's position as a follower of radical Islam has never been certain. On the one hand, he has always been a vocal opponent of Israel and a supporter of Palestinians. He has given financial aid to radical Muslim groups that engaged in terrorism. These actions brought him support from radical Islamic believers. On the other hand, the brand of Islam that Qaddafi preaches at home encourages his people to follow government rather than religious leaders.

Qaddafi warned Libyan Muslim leaders critical of the government not to speak out in opposition to him. Many people saw this as a way to prevent Muslim leaders from competing with the government for the people's loyalty, thus suppressing the leaders' power. This left Qaddafi and his regime as the sole authority in the country.

Some traditional Libyan Muslims consider Qaddafi a heretic (one who preaches dissenting religious beliefs). They say that he promotes his ideas on religious matters as accepted Islamic teachings. Many Muslim clerics (religious officials) and others feel Qaddafi's ideas on religion insult traditional Muslims.

CHAPTER 6

RELATIONS

LIFE IN LIBYA UNDER QADDAFI HAS CHANGED a great deal since he assumed control in 1969. Qaddafi claims to be dedicated to creating a nation that is centered on its citizens. Jamahiriya, a term coined by Qaddafi to describe Libya, means just that. But control has remained largely in the hands of Qaddafi and his administration. The growing number of opposition groups inside and outside of Libya suggest that the people's will is not being followed.

At the same time, Libya's position in the world has undergone some serious changes. It began as a poor, powerless country and grew into an international terrorist threat. There were times when it was applauded by its Arab neighbors, while being condemned by the Western world. At other times, the country was largely friendless, as other Arab and African countries were suspicious of Qaddafi's actions. In the twenty-first century, as Libya moves

AT HOME AND ABROAD

QADDAFI SPEAKS TO THE LIBYAN
press in front of a sculpture in Tripoli. It is a memorial to the 1986 U.S. bombing of Tripoli and shows a gold fist crushing a U.S. fighter plane.

back into the international community's good graces, Qaddafi's next move remains a mystery.

RETAINING CONTROL

Qaddafi's regime has been known for treating its critics harshly. Individual citizens, members of opposition groups, and journalists have been jailed or executed for speaking out against the government. Sometimes dissidents simply disappear. Even Libyans living outside the country could not be sure of their safety if they spoke against Qaddafi. He sent his agents to kill some of these people while they lived abroad.

Although Qaddafi ran Libya as he pleased for many years, his people gradually grew tired of his restrictions and his frequent changes of direction. In 1986 the United States dropped bombs on Libyan cities in retaliation for a terrorist bombing in West Germany. The attack caught the Libyan Army off guard, and the military could do little to combat U.S. fighter planes as they invaded Libya's airspace. While many countries around the world condemned the U.S. bombing, few Libyans expressed anger over the incident. The lack of preparedness of the armed forces left the Libyan military feeling disheartened.

THE NEED FOR REFORM

The U.S. attack and its aftermath prompted Qaddafi to make some changes to his regime. He seemed to realize that his citizens' lack of outrage over the bombings meant that they were dissatisfied with his rule. Over the next two years, he began to relax some of the government controls imposed during the preceding decades. He ordered the release of many political prisoners and the destruction of thousands of security files the government had assembled on Libyan citizens. He eased travel restrictions and returned confiscated passports to their owners.

OPERATION EL DORADO CANYON

In 1986, when the United States conducted an air strike, named Operation El Dorado Canyon, against the al-Azizya Barracks near Tripoli, Qaddafi's wife, Safia, was outraged about the assault on her family. She was quoted in the *Chicago Tribune* as saying, "I will kill him myself," if given the opportunity to meet the pilot responsible for destroying her home.

U.S. president Reagan said the air strikes were necessary because of terrorist activities in which Libya had engaged. In particular, Reagan claimed to have evidence that Libyans were responsible for bombing a West Berlin disco *(below)* on April 5, 1986.

Many felt that the air strikes on April 15, 1986, were personal in nature rather than a simple military strategy. The fact that Qaddafi's personal quarters were targeted indicates that Reagan might have been trying to assassinate the Libyan leader.

Qaddafi even announced changes to the judicial system. No longer were citizens subject to arrest for no reason. He assembled a list of specific crimes for which people could be arrested.

The government also drafted the Great Green Charter of Human Rights of the Jamahiriyan Era. On the surface, this document guaranteed extensive human rights protections to the Libyans. It allowed private property and granted the right to an attorney to those arrested for crimes. But many of the Green Charter's provisions were very general. It left decisions about what the charter meant up to the government.

The document appeared to say what Libyan citizens wanted to hear, but in practice, it was not a significant step forward for human rights. The regime retained power as before. Opposition to the government's policies was still considered treason. The penalty for those convicted of treason is death.

Qaddafi himself often speaks out against the government. Since he has no official position in it, he is able to add to his public appeal by criticizing governmental policies that dissatisfy them. He can place the blame for failed policies on others, thereby maintaining his own popularity. Even so, his role as Libya's undisputed leader is well known.

By the late 1980s and into the 1990s, Qaddafi was having more difficulty quieting citizen unrest. People had to rely on the government for their food and other goods since the country was still largely supplied by state-run stores. The government was not as efficient as the free market when it came to mastering supply and demand. Store shelves were often bare, leaving people with little choice but to try to obtain goods through an illegal black market.

Life was difficult for the average Libyan by the late 1990s. Their government-set wages had not increased in twenty years. Qaddafi's involvement with international terrorism had caused other nations to cut off diplomatic and economic ties with the nation. This meant that Libya could not import goods such as food and medicine from Western European countries and the United States. Even when Libyans had money in their wallets, goods were scarce. People were not able to travel out of the country for tourism or to study. Attempts made by the Qaddafi regime to involve citizens in economic reforms had been a failure. Libyans mistrusted their government.

STEELWORKERS WAIT FOR REPAIRS AT A FACTORY IN TRIPOLI IN 1992.
Libyan industry suffered because many countries, in protest of Qaddafi's support for international terrorism, refused to buy Libyan products or to sell goods and equipment to Libya.

ECONOMIC CHANGES

There had been little continuity in the country's economic policies since the 1969 revolution. The regime had confiscated (taken) private property, outlawed private business ownership, and forced citizens to give up their savings when the nation introduced a new currency. As a result, most citizens were not eager to accept any new changes implemented by Qaddafi's government. They had been subject to their leader's whims for too long to be enthusiastic about any new promises or plans.

A sharp drop in oil prices in the 1980s meant that Libya had less money to spend. The number of government employees was reduced, partly because of the country's lack of funds to pay so many workers. Even government utilities such as water soon became more expensive for consumers. By cutting back the size of government and providing fewer goods and services to the public, Qaddafi placed more emphasis on private businesses. The ultimate result was to strengthen the private sector as the public sector weakened.

The drop in oil prices caused a drop in military spending. During the early 1980s, Libya imported billions of dollars worth of weapons to equip its growing military. By the early 1990s, that amount had dropped into the millions of dollars, and by the mid-1990s, Libya imported no weapons at all.

The economic reforms attempted by Qaddafi to solve his nation's problems were not successful in turning the economy around. The sanctions imposed by the United States and United Nations undermined Qaddafi's attempts to privatize the economy. In addition, there was so little confidence in the Libyan economy

A GILDED PORTRAIT OF QADDAFI WELCOMES VISITORS TO AN OIL
and gas processing company near Tripoli. Government dependence on oil revenue
caused a severe economic downturn during the late 1980s.

that U.S. dollars became the popular medium of exchange. Clearly,
stronger measures were called for.

FRIENDS AND NEIGHBORS

Shortly after Qaddafi took over Libya, he announced that one of
his chief goals was the pursuit of Arab unity. Similarly, a number of
European nations had begun to discuss joining together, and some
years later these discussions led to the creation of the European

Union (EU). The EU nations form a powerful, effective trading block, and many of them even share a common currency called the Euro. Qaddafi pledged a great deal of his country's oil revenue to establishing a similar Arab unity.

Qaddafi had begun the task with Egypt's President Nasser, but Nasser died in 1970. As later negotiations with Egypt failed, Qaddafi approached other Arab nations. But these negotiations did not turn out well. Throughout the 1970s, Qaddafi had disagreements with many of his neighbors, including Tunisia and Sudan, as well as continuing tensions with Egypt. Libya also had a lengthy border dispute with its southern neighbor Chad.

It was frustrating for Qaddafi that the other Arab nations were not as committed to unity as he was. He eventually gave up on his dream after decades without success. A combination of factors might have been to blame for the failure of Qaddafi's plans for unity. Some Arab leaders, used to having complete control of their countries, might not have liked the idea of working so closely with fellow heads of state in the region. Unity would have required them to give up some of their nations' sovereignty, or independence. It might have meant checking with other countries about foreign relations or even domestic economic decisions.

Qaddafi's own reputation for unpredictable behavior might have made his neighbors reluctant to become too closely tied to him. His refusal to turn over the terrorist suspects from the 1972 slayings at the Munich Olympics brought condemnation from around the globe. He made enemies in both Arab and Western nations, which might have made other nations' leaders nervous.

Other Arab leaders have not always taken Qaddafi as seriously as he would like. Perhaps his reputation for being too erratic, or changeable, damaged his chances at working closely with fellow

A SUDANESE MAN PICKS THROUGH THE WRECKAGE OF HIS HOUSE AFTER
Libyan bombers attacked border towns in Sudan during its border war with Chad in the 1970s.

world leaders. The Arab people, on the other hand, were usually more generous toward him than their leaders, primarily because of his strong support of the Palestinian cause.

Qaddafi decided to turn his attention to uniting his sub-Saharan neighbors, reflecting Libya's position between the Arab world and Africa. In 1990 he was instrumental in forming the

African Union, an organization with representatives from most African countries. It works to settle African problems and promote African interests.

STATE SUPPORT OF TERRORISM

The relationship between the United States and Libya was strained for many years of Qaddafi's rule. At times the two nations went beyond unfriendliness to outright confrontation. One key problem was Qaddafi's support of the PLO's efforts to force Israel out of Palestinian-claimed lands. The United States opposed such violence against their Israeli allies and supported Israel's right to the land.

The Libyan government defended its position on Israel. In 1989 Libyan foreign minister Jadallah Azzuz al-Talhi complained, "The United States knows very well where the chemical and nuclear weapons are in the Middle East. The United States knows that the Zionist state [Israel] is an arsenal of chemical and nuclear weapons, yet has not raised a single question about it. Furthermore, is it not Washington which gives Israel the aid and the capabilities needed for producing such weapons and is it not the Zionist state which, with U.S. backing and knowledge, refuses to abide by the international laws and treaties concluded in connection with these types of weapons?"

The United States had long suspected Libya of supporting terrorist groups around the world. It specifically condemned Libya's support for the PLO in Palestine, and it also condemned the nation's general support for terrorism worldwide. The U.S. government believed Libya was giving financial support to more than two dozen terrorist groups by the late 1980s. Because of Qaddafi's terrorist activities, President Reagan called him the "mad dog of the Middle East."

Libya was included in the U.S. State Department's list of state sponsors of terrorism in 1979. Libya had infuriated U.S. leaders by hosting a visit from Cuban Socialist President Fidel Castro in 1977.

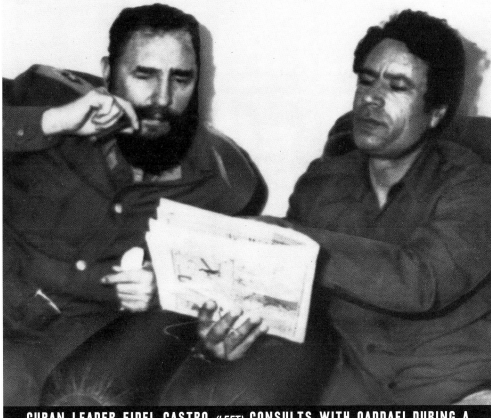

CUBAN LEADER FIDEL CASTRO *(LEFT)* **CONSULTS WITH QADDAFI DURING A** meeting of Libyan and Cuban delegates in Tripoli in 1977. The United States feared an alliance between Libya and the Soviet Union, a political and military enemy of the United States.

Reagan's administration tried to claim that Libya was an ally of the Soviet Union (USSR). Since both Libya and the USSR were Socialist nations, it was not difficult to cast the two countries in a similar light for U.S. audiences. The United States and the Soviet Union had been involved in a decades-long Cold War (1945–1991), and most Americans feared the threat posed by its powerful enemy. Linking Libya to the USSR was an effective way for Reagan to encourage Americans' distrust of Libya and Qaddafi.

At the same time, Libya was involved in the politics of its African neighbors, including Chad. Author Ronald Bruce St. John summed up Libya's situation this way: "Libya rests on the periphery [edge] of three worlds—Arab, Africa, and Mediterranean. This location has given it some flexibility as to where it will play a role as well as creating uncertainty as to exactly where it belongs." Because of Libya's geography and politics, it found itself belonging to three different regions, while not being entirely a part of any of them.

Given Libya's political climate, it came as no surprise when the U.S. oil company Exxon removed its operations from Libya in 1981. Shortly afterward, the United States barred the import of all Libyan oil, and it was not long before the entire huge U.S. oil market was closed to Libya.

In Great Britain, Yvonne Fletcher, a London police officer, was killed outside London's Libyan Embassy in 1984. The London police had been keeping the peace during an anti-Qaddafi demonstration outside the embassy. Shots fired from inside the embassy killed the police officer. The Libyan government never admitted responsibility, and those inside the building were whisked out of the country. This incident cast a shadow over relations between Libya and Great Britain.

In 1986 Qaddafi's terrorist involvement brought on the

bombing raid by U.S. forces that included the military barracks at al-Azizya. In general, Americans responded to the bombing favorably, but many outside the United States were outraged by the attacks. Especially in the Arab world, Reagan's decision to bomb Libya was viewed as unwarranted. Several countries, including the Soviet Union and Afghanistan, canceled meetings with U.S. diplomats in protest.

Despite the opposition from abroad, the U.S. bombing had a lasting impact on Qaddafi. He spoke against Reagan's action, yet he knew that the incident had hurt morale in Libya. His military was disheartened by the ease with which the United States had attacked them.

"We must all work to stamp out the scourge of terrorism that in the Middle East makes war an ever-present threat."

–U.S. president Ronald Reagan, in a 1982 speech to the British Parliament

Although his involvement with terrorist activities was causing Libya to be shunned by the international community, Qaddafi did not call a halt to it. In 1988 his country was tied to the terrorist

POLICE OFFICERS GUARD THE WRECKAGE OF THE U.S. AIRLINER BOMBED over Lockerbie, Scotland, in 1988.

bombing of a U.S. airliner over Lockerbie, Scotland. And in 1989, the French government accused Libya of bombing a French plane, killing all 170 people aboard.

On August 2, 1990, U.S. president George H. W. Bush outlined his nation's military strategy for the future. The Soviet Union, which had been the United States' greatest threat for many years, was collapsing, but this did not mean that the U.S. military would shrink in size. Bush described a world full of unpredictable dangers from other nations. He explained his view that because countries were developing weapons of mass destruction and could easily threaten the American way of life, the U.S. military must stay strong and ready to fight.

LOCKERBIE DISASTER

On December 21, 1988, Pan American (Pan Am) flight 103 exploded over Lockerbie, Scotland. The plane had taken off from London's Heathrow Airport bound for New York City. Plastic explosives in the cargo hold blew up, causing the plane to come apart in midair. All 259 people aboard the plane died, as did 11 people on the ground hit by falling debris. The vast majority of the airplane's passengers were Americans.

A criminal investigation was conducted by both U.S. and British officials. The result was that U.S. and Scottish prosecutors indicted two Libyans, one a government intelligence officer and the other a security officer for Libyan Arab Airlines, on murder charges. An indictment means a court has decided that there is enough evidence that the defendants must stand trial.

Despite the charges, Colonel Qaddafi refused to turn the men over for trial. This led the United Nations to impose sanctions against Libya. The sanctions included a ban on arms sales and international restrictions on people traveling in and out of Libya. Negotiations continued until 1999. At that time, Qaddafi finally agreed to allow the men to be tried, but not in a Scottish court because of the risk that the men might not receive a fair trial. They were both tried in the Netherlands.

The result of the trial was that Abdel Basset Ali al-Megrahi, the Libyan security officer, was convicted in 2001 and is currently serving time in a Scottish prison. He claims that he is innocent. The other defendant was found not guilty and was set free. Negotiations following Megrahi's conviction resulted in Libya promising to pay millions of dollars to the families of each victim. With this payment, the UN dropped its sanctions completely.

Bush's strategy became known as the Rogue Doctrine. The Bush administration and the Clinton administration that came after it identified the rogue nations that posed significant threats to U.S. security. The United States accused these nations—including Libya, Iran, and Iraq—of being ruled by unpredictable leaders who supported terrorism. The description of Libya as a rogue nation suggested that the U.S. military was ready at a moment's notice to invade the country if its actions were seen as hostile.

ECONOMIC SANCTIONS

Libya suffered under international economic sanctions throughout the 1980s and 1990s. The United States closed its embassy in Tripoli and refused to allow the importation of Libyan oil or products made from Libyan oil. This did some damage to Libya's oil industry, but a number of markets still existed around the world. The fact that the United States also refused to sell its products to Libya caused greater difficulty for Qaddafi's country.

Libya had taken over the Libyan oil fields of U.S. companies years before. By the 1990s, the equipment in those oil fields was in need of repair. Under the U.S. sanctions, no parts or manpower could be sent to Libya, and the oil fields fell into further disrepair.

After the U.S. bombing of Tripoli and Benghazi in 1986, it seemed for a brief time that Qaddafi was interested in reducing the tension between Libya and Western nations. However, the explosion of the Pan Am airliner over Lockerbie, Scotland, in 1988 brought relations between Libya and both the United States and Great Britain to a new low. The explosion of a French airliner over

Niger the following year disrupted Libyan relations with France. When the United States and Great Britain charged two Libyans in the Pan Am bombing, Qaddafi refused to turn the men over for trial. Similarly, the French indicted four Libyans in the airline bombing over Niger, but the Libyan government refused to turn over those men to France.

In the wake of Libya's lack of cooperation, the United Nations Security Council passed a resolution that imposed sanctions in 1992. The sanctions meant that UN members severely limited imports to and exports from Libya. International flights into Libya were banned, and no arms could be sold to the country.

Libya's economic situation grew worse throughout the mid to late 1990s. For example, tourism had the potential to bring in billions of badly needed dollars to the Libyan economy, but the international sanctions prevented leisure travel into the country from most nations around the world.

It is impossible to identify the precise impact of international sanctions on the Libyan people. Libya is reluctant to provide such information since it might cast the government and its policies in an unfavorable light. Qaddafi and the individuals who made up his regime continued to have sufficient food and medicine despite sanctions. The average Libyan citizen might not have been so fortunate. Shortages of medical supplies plagued the country during the years the sanctions were in place.

By comparing Libya to other countries living under sanctions, it is possible to estimate the sanctions' impact. If Libya suffered nearly as much as Iraq, which faced U.S. and UN sanctions starting in 1990, then many thousands of deaths might have resulted from the punishment imposed by the international community against Qaddafi's regime.

Using data from the World Bank (an institution providing financial aid to developing countries), political scientist John T. Rourke said, "The year before sanctions were imposed on Iraq, its child mortality rates and those of its neighbors [including Turkey, Iran, Jordan, Saudi Arabia, Syria, and Kuwait] were about the same. By 2002, the last full year of the sanctions, the child mortality rate in Iraq had risen 51 percent and was four times higher than the average for its neighbors, whose child mortality rate has declined 59 percent. Whether the sanctions were the cause of the higher mortality rate or whether it was the unwillingness of the Iraqi regime to redistribute funds away from its military to child nutrition and health care is still being debated. But there is little doubt that without the sanctions, 15,000 or more Iraqi children would probably have lived past age five than did." Libya may have suffered the same sorts of child mortality rates.

THAWING RELATIONS

As a new millennium approached, Qaddafi's regime seemed interested in making significant changes to its standing in the international community. Libya's economic troubles could be relieved if the country were removed from the U.S. list of state sponsors of terrorism. If that were to happen, greater markets for Libya's oil and oil products would open up. It could once again import technologies that would update and repair its antiquated oil industry. Western companies might again invest in Libya, something they had avoided since the Libyan government had taken control of private assets in the 1970s.

With the prize of economic expansion in mind, Libya tried a new approach in dealing with the international community. In 1999 Libya finally agreed to turn over the two suspects for trial in the Lockerbie airline bombing, and the United Nations suspended its economic sanctions.

The United States, however, still maintained its sanctions against Libya. But this was less effective because the United States was one of the few countries in the world that still refused to deal with Qaddafi. The sanctions, including a travel ban to Libya from the United States, were still in place when Qaddafi publicly denounced the September 11, 2001, terrorist attacks in the United States. He went on to approve of the ensuing U.S. invasion of Afghanistan.

The only issue holding up reconciliation between Libya and the United States was Libya's attempts to develop chemical and nuclear

"Irrespective of the conflict with America, it is a human duty to show sympathy with the American people and be with them at these horrifying and awesome events which are bound to awaken human conscience."

—Muammar al-Qaddafi in a September 11, 2001, press conference on the terrorist attacks of that day

QADDAFI LISTENS TO DELIBERATIONS AT THE AL-AZIZIA PALACE IN TRIPOLI
in 2003. That year, he closed all of Libya's nuclear, chemical, and biological weapons programs in response to international pressure.

weapons technology. When Libya finally signed an agreement in 2003 that promised to end its programs, it removed the last obstacle to peace between the two countries. U.S. inspectors were allowed full access to Libya and assisted in disarming and removing items related to the creation of chemical and nuclear weapons.

In 2004 the United States lifted the travel ban to Libya for Americans. Soon afterward, representatives from the U.S. Congress visited the country. This led to the resumption of full diplomatic relations between the two countries.

The improved relations between Libya and the rest of the world quickly took hold and brought improved economic prospects for Qaddafi's people. Western businesses—especially oil companies—

made their way to Libya. Qaddafi was even invited to an official meeting of the European Union in Brussels, Belgium, in 2004. Protesters outside the meeting pointed out the continued persistent human rights abuses in Libya.

Since travel restrictions have eased and borders have opened up for educational and scientific pursuits, a lack of fluency in other languages may be a problem for modern Libyans. Anticipating this, Qaddafi's regime added English and French to the Libyan school curriculum in 2004. It will be some time, however, before many Libyans are fluent enough to conduct business in those languages.

If Libya continues along a positive course with the rest of the world, its people have a great deal to gain. In July 2006, for example, the U.S. Department of Health and Human Services met with Libyan officials in Tripoli. At the meeting, the United States pledged $1 million to help Libya with disease control. The representatives explored other issues during the meeting, including water resources, education, health, and the environment. Both sides also pledged to improve passage for scientists and students traveling between the two countries. This suggests that after years of isolation, Libyans can finally be included in the shared resources of the world's scientific and educational communities.

BULGARIAN NURSES' TRIAL

Although Qaddafi's relationship with the rest of the world seemed to be improving, it was far from trouble free. One lingering problem was the HIV trial of a Palestinian doctor and five Bulgarian nurses in Libya. At the trial in 2004, evidence against the six accused included a confession by one of the nurses. She said that she had been given HIV-tainted blood by a British friend and that she and her co-workers had used the blood to infect Libyan children under their care. The Libyan prosecutors produced a videotape of a search at the nurse's apartment in Benghazi that showed the vials of tainted blood.

Kristiyana Vulcheva, the nurse who confessed, said that her confession had been the result of torture. Experts from around the globe testified that the conditions at al-Fatah Children's Hospital—the facility in Benghazi where the doctor and five nurses practiced—were unhygienic and that the reuse of needles and other supplies could easily have spread the HIV virus throughout the hospital. Luc Montagnier, one of the researchers responsible for discovering the HIV virus decades ago, testified that the virus strain that had sickened the Libyan children had been present before the Bulgarian nurses' arrival at the hospital. That would mean the nurses probably hadn't infected the children.

Despite the claims of torture and the extensive scientific evidence, a court in Benghazi convicted the six health-care workers in May 2004. They were sentenced to death. Negotiations continued among the United States, Libya, Bulgaria, and the European Union to free the workers from Libyan prison. The Western nations offered to treat the HIV-positive children and provide money to their families for the children's care. Libya asked for $10 million per child, which was what that country had promised to the families of the Lockerbie terrorist bombing victims. Bulgaria balked at the $10 million figure, saying it could not afford such a steep price.

The Western nations were unable to reach an agreement with Libya for the health-care workers' release. They remained in Libya and were granted a retrial. In December 2006, a court in Tripoli upheld the guilty verdict and the death sentences. Attorneys for the accused promised to bring the case to Libya's Supreme Court.

HIV IN LIBYA

In 1998 Libyan authorities arrested five Bulgarian nurses and one Palestinian doctor and charged them with purposely infecting hundreds of patients with HIV, the virus that causes AIDS. What came to be known as the Bulgarian Nurses' Trial drew attention to a growing HIV problem in Libya. Experts who testified at the trial believed that the HIV cases among more than 450 Libyan children arose from poor hygiene practices at Benghazi's al-Fatah Children's Hospital. They all agreed that the infections did not stem from any crime on the part of the foreign nurses or doctor. According to an article in the *New England Journal of Medicine*, Nobel Prize winner Richard Roberts said, "The Libyan government doesn't want to admit that their hospital had a problem with hygiene that spread HIV."

According to experts, a likely source of the children's HIV infections could be the more than one million sub-Saharan Africans who live and work in Libya. They are treated in the Libyan health-care system while residing in the country. In some sub-Saharan countries, HIV rates have reached 20 percent of the population. Needles and other medical equipment had been reused at the Benghazi hospital, and it is quite possible that blood from an infected person could have quickly spread through a hospital ward. It appears that Libya was reluctant to admit that it has its own AIDS crisis. The Qaddafi regime preferred to lay the blame on an act of alleged bioterrorism by foreign health-care workers.

International rights groups, the United States, and Western European nations complained about the verdicts in both trials. The *New York Times* quoted French lawyer and defense team member Emmanuel Altit when he discussed the 2006 decision. He said, "The question of torture by electricity, proof that the nurses have been beaten, sexually harassed, kept for six months without contact, the question of fabricated [made-up] evidence, none of this was discussed at all. The court refused to hear our experts." Finally, in 2007 the six were released after successful secret negotiations, led by Cécilia Sarkozy, the former wife of the president of France.

FIVE BULGARIAN HEALTH-CARE WORKERS AND ONE PALESTINIAN DOCTOR
accused of infecting Libyan children with HIV attend their trial in Benghazi in 2007.

SANCTIONS AND HIV

When the international community was enforcing sanctions on Libya, it was difficult for the country to obtain medical supplies and medicine. In 1998, when the five Bulgarian nurses and a Palestinian doctor working in Libya were accused of deliberately infecting hundreds of Libyan children with the HIV virus, international public health experts identified poor hygiene at the hospital as the most likely source of the infections. They pointed out that needles and other equipment were reused on different children.

It may be that the children were infected as a direct result of the lack of supplies. If fresh needles and equipment had been readily available, perhaps needles would not have been reused. If fresh equipment had been used on each patient, perhaps the virus would not have been passed along.

LINGERING DOUBTS

When the United States resumed trade and diplomatic relations with Libya in 2004, it appeared that Muammar al-Qaddafi had finally decided he wanted to be on friendly terms with the rest of the world. He publicly rejected terrorism. He gave up his country's weapons of mass destruction (WMD) programs and even allowed inspectors access to verify that his research had been dismantled. He again allowed foreign companies to do business within Libya.

IN 2004 QADDAFI VISITED BRUSSELS, BELGIUM, AND MET WITH MEMBERS
of the Belgian Federal Parliament. It was his first visit to Europe since 1989.

There are a variety of theories about why Qaddafi abandoned his WMD programs and softened his stance against much of the world, the West in particular. One possibility is that he realized Libya's continued isolation would result in a never-ending spiral of economic difficulties. If conditions grew bad enough, it could result in his people rising up against him. Only by opening up his country could Qaddafi hope to have economic sanctions lifted, leading to improvements in Libya's economy.

Another theory is that after the United States invaded Iraq and removed Saddam Hussein from power in 2003, Qaddafi feared he might be next. Rather than risk a fate similar to Saddam's, Qaddafi chose to reject his earlier hard-line position on a number of issues and enter into a more cooperative relationship with the United States. Of course, this explanation does not address the reasons behind Qaddafi's cooperation in 1999, which led to the UN and Great Britain lifting their sanctions. The United States did not invade Iraq until 2003, years after Libya had turned over the Lockerbie bombing suspects and made peace with Britain.

While Qaddafi might be sincere about his decision to be a more responsible citizen of the world, many remain skeptical. After decades of running a dictatorship with a firm hand and often operating outside the standards of international law, many outsiders view Qaddafi's motives with suspicion.

While Qaddafi has made some changes in international relations, he has shown little improvement in his human rights record at home. He did release some political prisoners. One prisoner

"The main problem the regime [in Libya] has is to build the trust of the people. There is a lack of credibility for the regime. When anything comes from the state, even if it is good, they think they are bluffing."

—Giumma Attigha, lawyer and leader of

a Tripoli human rights committee, 2007

released was Fathi al-Jahmi, who had been arrested in 2002 for speaking out against the government. At the same time, Qaddafi has arrested hundreds more, and he rearrested al-Jahmi in 2004. According to the 2007 World Report of Human Rights Watch—an international human rights organization—al-Jahmi was being tried for violating a Libyan law against forming political parties. If convicted, he could face a death sentence.

"Libya wants the world to think it's changed, but Fathi al-Jahmi's unlawful detention and systematic mistreatment are a disgrace for a country that wants acceptance by the world community."

–Joe Stork, acting Middle East director at Human Rights Watch, 2008

Human Rights Watch cites other evidence that suggests Qaddafi might not have truly reformed. The media in Libya remains strictly controlled by the government, with no private ownership of media outlets. More than one thousand inmates died in an uprising in 1996 at Abu Salim prison in Tripoli. The uprising began with prisoners protesting living conditions. It has yet to be investigated. Another protest occurred in 2006 at the same prison, resulting in one fatality. Many examples of continuing human rights abuses are listed by Human Rights Watch and other observers of Libyan society.

Perhaps Qaddafi's attempts at reform only involved foreign relations and are not meant to modernize Libyan society. It is also possible that a massive shift in the leader's practices will take time. Some improvements have been made in the new millennium, and it might be important to reward these in hopes that they will lead to more. While the revolution that brought Qaddafi to power only lasted a few hours, changes that can permanently alter his legacy could take years.

CHAPTER 7

WHAT HAPPENS

LIBYA'S EFFORTS AT ECONOMIC IMPROVEMENT and international cooperation went hand in hand with the introduction of new faces in Qaddafi's regime. Qaddafi's son Saif al-Islam al-Qaddafi began to take a more active role in government affairs. He was responsible for announcing a series of reforms while he attended an international economic summit in 2005.

It is interesting, however, that Saif al-Islam did not appear to have any authority to promise reforms. He had not received approval from the General People's Congress to speak on behalf of the government, and like his father, he did not hold any formal position in the Libyan government. This calls into question whether real changes are being made in Qaddafi's regime.

Former Libyan prime minister Shukri Ghanem was present at the economic summit with Qaddafi's son, but some doubt that even

SHUKRI GHANEM *(LEFT)* **AND SHELL OIL CHIEF EXECUTIVE LINDA COOK** *(RIGHT)*
sign an agreement on a joint liquid gas exploration operation in 2008. After serving as Libya's prime minister, Ghanem became the Libyan oil minister.

the prime minister had any actual power. Ghanem favored reform, but the Libyan government removed him from office in March 2006. His views promoting the continuing privatization of Libyan businesses often ran counter to other members of the government, who preferred to remain within a Socialist system.

A new generation is coming into power in Libya. This is true in the country as a whole, as well as in the top levels of the government. In 2003 Libya's unemployment rate stood at 30 percent. This large, young, unemployed population required an expansion of the economy to create jobs. One way to create jobs is to invite more foreign investment in business and in the oil industry.

In 2004 the GPC allowed 360 more businesses to be privatized. This move never would have been possible in the 1970s, when Libya was governed under the strict Socialist terms of *The Green Book*. Also, in 2004 Libya announced that it would allow new exploration for oil by a number of foreign companies.

How much more successful will the reforms of the new millennium be, compared to those that were attempted in the late 1980s and 1990s? It is too early to say for sure, but they have some chance of success. In the 1980s and 1990s, Libya was still an isolated country, shunned by much of the world for its terrorist activities. With economic sanctions lifted, the country now has access to investment money, technology, and markets.

A NEW ERA FOR LIBYA?

While the government is still tightly controlled by Qaddafi and his inner circle, the economic prospects for Libyans seem to be brighter. Qaddafi might be grooming his son, Saif al-Islam, to take his place someday. Saif al-Islam, who was born in 1972, still holds no formal position in the Libyan government. Of course, neither does his father, and that has not stopped the senior Qaddafi from leading his nation for decades.

SAIF AL-ISLAM AL-QADDAFI outlines changes to Libya's constitution in a 2007 speech. He stressed that his father would remain in control.

On the surface, Saif al-Islam seems to be a force for change. He speaks openly of the new path that the Libyan government must follow. During an interview with the *New York Times* in 2004, he said, "Democracy is the future. . . . The whole world is heading toward democracy." During the interview, he denied that he was being prepared to take his father's place. He said of his father's job as the unofficial Libyan leader, "It is not inherited."[25]

In addition to championing the need for democracy—in a country that still bans political parties opposed to the government—Saif al-Islam also works for human rights. For example, he investigated the charges of torture that were brought by the Bulgarian nurses and Palestinian doctor being held in the HIV trial beginning in 1999. He founded an international charitable organization, and he was involved in the negotiations to reach a financial settlement with the families of the victims from the Lockerbie jetliner bombing in 1988.

But Saif al-Islam also defends the Libyan government. For example, when asked about any resistance or political opposition to the existing regime, Saif claimed, "We don't have an opposition—

> *"Society needs to have independent media to highlight corruption, cheating and falsification."*
>
> —Saif al-Islam al-Qaddafi,
>
> announcing plans to reform Libyan media, 2007

there is no opposition." But an Internet search of anti-Qaddafi websites proves otherwise. There are a number of groups outside Libya opposed to the leader's rule, including the National Conference for the Libyan Opposition and the National Front for the Salvation of Libya.

Some observers don't think that Saif al-Islam is in line to succeed his father. They say it is Qaddafi's daughter, Aisha, who will be her father's choice. As a lawyer, she was a part of former Iraqi president Saddam Hussein's defense team in Saddam's 2005 trial in Iraq. Aisha is known throughout Libya as a modern woman who lives according to traditional Islamic principles.

It is thought that naming a woman to fill Qaddafi's shoes would be an appealing move for him to make. It would be a typical one for Libya's eccentric leader. Throughout the nearly four decades since Qaddafi and his men overturned the monarchy, Libyans and the world have come to expect the unexpected from him. He supported terrorism for many years but now opposes it. He banned private business ownership under the terms of *The Green Book*, but now he encourages it. He even explored weapons of mass destruction but has since forsaken them.

The future for Libya is in question. The country appears to be on a path toward full membership in the international community. However, Qaddafi has changed his mind before about what he feels is in his country's best interests.

TURNING OVER A NEW LEAF

Has Qaddafi really turned over a new leaf? Is he honestly dedicated to international cooperation, particularly with the United States and Western Europe? Appearances suggest that he is. Allowing inspectors into Libya to search for and remove materials for weapons of mass destruction was a step in the right direction. However, other circumstances are less promising.

In 2004 two people were accused of planning to assassinate Saudi Arabia's Crown Prince Abdullah. One of those accused was a Libyan intelligence officer. Although Qaddafi denied any connection to the plot, it is widely known that he has little love for the leaders of Saudi Arabia's government. Qaddafi has accused Saudi Arabia's leaders of giving money to Libyan groups that oppose him.

Only time will tell if Qaddafi's efforts at reform, both in his country and with the outside world, are sincere. His behavior over the past forty years is reason enough to keep observers guessing.

WHO'S WHO?

YVONNE FLETCHER (1959–1984) This British police officer was killed outside the Libyan Embassy in London on April 17, 1984. She was shot from inside the embassy, apparently by a Libyan since only embassy personnel were inside. She and other officers were stationed outside the embassy that day because dissidents opposed to Qaddafi were protesting. The incident ended diplomatic relations between Libya and Great Britain.

SHUKRI GHANEM (1942–) Ghanem was Libyan prime minister from June 2003 until March 2006. He was a reform-minded leader who was responsible for encouraging free-market changes in his country. He took many state-owned companies and placed them in private hands. He is also given credit for helping end Libya's many years of strained relations with the international community. It is believed that he lost his position because his reforms were controversial within the government, although those in the private sector approved of his actions. In 2006 he became Libya's oil minister.

IDRIS I (1889–1983) The grandson of Sayyid Mohammad bin Ali al-Sanusi, he was the first and only Libyan king. Idris offered aid to the British during World War II. He ruled from Libya's independence in 1951 until Qaddafi's military coup in 1969. Idris was out of the country during the coup. He never returned to Libya but instead lived out his life in Egypt.

FATHI AL-JAHMI (1942–) Identified by Human Rights Watch's World Report 2007 as the best-known political prisoner in Libya, he has been held in custody without formal charges since 2004. As of early 2007, he was still awaiting trial for attempting to set up opposition political parties in Libya. He could face the death penalty if convicted.

GAMAL ABDEL NASSER (1918–1970) Nasser was Egyptian president from 1954 to 1970 and was Qaddafi's hero. While president of Egypt, he worked toward unity among Arab nations. He also fought Western influences within the Arab world and brought a form of Socialism to his country. These causes were all taken up by Qaddafi when he became Libya's leader.

AISHA AL-QADDAFI (1977–) Aisha is Muammar al-Qaddafi's only daughter. She is a lawyer, who some believe will be named by her father to take his place as Libya's leader when he steps down or dies.

HANNA AL-QADDAFI (1985?–1986) This young girl was killed by the U.S. bombing raids over Tripoli on April 15, 1986. Qaddafi claimed she was his adopted daughter, but there is some speculation about the accuracy of the statement. It has been suggested that she was adopted by him after her death.

SAIF AL-ISLAM AL-QADDAFI (1972–) Saif is the second son of Muammar al-Qaddafi. Many believe he will be the probable successor to his father. He currently holds no formal position in the Libyan government. He runs the Gaddafi International Foundation for Charity Associations and has spoken on behalf of Libya at gatherings of international leaders.

RONALD REAGAN (1911–2004) Reagan was president of the United States from 1981 to 1989. During the Reagan administration, relations between the United States and Libya were severed. Reagan authorized stiff sanctions against Libya for its support of terrorism and ordered the April 15, 1986, bombing raids on Tripoli and Benghazi.

SAYYID MOHAMMAD BIN ALI AL-SANUSI (1787–1860) This Libyan religious leader started the Sanusi Muslim religious order in 1837. Many Libyans followed the teachings of this order, which recommends a simple life and a liberal interpretation of the Quran.

KRISTIYANA VULCHEVA (1959–) She is one of the five Bulgarian nurses accused of infecting more than 450 Libyan children with HIV in 1998. Although she confessed to the crime while in a Libyan prison, she later said that she had been tortured into making the statements. Along with five other foreign health-care workers, she was convicted of the crimes in Libyan courts and faced the death penalty. They were freed in 2007.

TIMELINE

1911 Italy invades and gains control over key cities in what would one day become Libya.

1945 Following its defeat in World War II, Italy loses control of Libya.

1951 The United Kingdom of Libya declares that it is an independent state. King Idris I heads the monarchy.

1959 Vast oil reserves are discovered in Libya's Cyrenaica region by the U.S. oil company Esso (later called ExxonMobil).

1969 A military coup by Captain Muammar al-Qaddafi and a group of other young military officers overthrows the Libyan monarchy.

1972 Libya is accused of involvement in the murder of Israeli athletes at the Munich Summer Olympics.

1977 Qaddafi renames Libya the Socialist People's Libyan Arab Jamahiriya.

1979 The U.S. State Department adds Libya to its list of countries that engage in state-sponsored terrorism.

1980 Qaddafi orders the deaths of "stray dogs," Libyan dissidents who are living outside the country.

1981 The National Front for the Salvation of Libya is formed. It opposes Qaddafi and seeks to overthrow his government.

1984 British police officer Yvonne Fletcher is shot and killed by someone inside the Libyan Embassy in London while she is on duty during a demonstration.

1986 Three people, including two U.S. soldiers, are killed when a bomb destroys a West Berlin disco. Libyan terrorists are blamed. In retaliation, U.S. president Ronald Reagan orders air strikes against targets in Libya, including the barracks where Qaddafi's family was staying.

1988   Pan Am Flight 103 explodes over Lockerbie, Scotland, killing all 259 passengers. An investigation later reveals that a Libyan intelligence officer is likely one of those responsible.

1990   Under the leadership of Qaddafi, the Surt Declaration calls for the establishment of the African Union.

1992   The United Nations Security Council passes a resolution that Libya must surrender its citizens who are charged with blowing up the Pan Am plane or face international sanctions, but Libya refuses.

1999   Libya agrees to turn over Lockerbie bombing suspects, and the UN suspends sanctions against Libya.

2001   One of the Libyan Pan Am bombing suspects is found guilty, while the other is found not guilty.

2003   Libya agrees to pay each of the Lockerbie victims' families $10 million in compensation. The UN cancels sanctions against Libya. Libya announces its plans to end weapons of mass destruction programs.

2004   The United States lifts economic sanctions and restores diplomatic relations with Libya.

2005   U.S. companies obtain licenses for oil exploration in Libya. Qaddafi's government announces new plans to further liberalize the country's economy.

2006   A second verdict is issued against five Bulgarian nurses and one Palestinian doctor in the Libyan HIV trial. The six defendants are again sentenced to death.

2007   The five Bulgarian nurses and the Palestinian doctor are freed through international intervention.

2008   Libya takes over the one-month rotating presidency of the UN Security Council.

GLOSSARY

Amazonian Guard: a group of highly trained women who serve as personal bodyguards to Muammar al-Qaddafi

Communism: a political and economic model based on the idea of common, rather than private, property. In a Communist system, the government controls capital and distributes it equally among citizens. The system is based on the writings of Karl Marx and Friedrich Engels.

coup d'état: a French term that refers to the overthrow of an existing government in favor of a new one

disappeared: victims of a dictatorship who are arrested and secretly detained, tortured, executed, and disposed of, with all records of their arrest and murder destroyed or concealed

dissidents: people who oppose an existing government and use protests or other means to remove it from power or work for reforms

General People's Congress (GPC): the national-level government body that is responsible for passing laws and establishing policies for the entire nation of Libya. It also selects members of the General People's Committee, which leads national government departments.

Great Man-Made River Project: a large, expensive project that pipes water from underground aquifers deep in the Sahara to Libya's Mediterranean coastal areas

Islam: a religion founded in the seventh century A.D. based on the teachings of the prophet Muhammad. Islam has two major sects, Shiite and Sunni. About 90 percent of all Muslims belong to the Sunni sect. The holy book of Islam is the Quran.

Jamahiriya: an Arabic word coined by Qaddafi to describe the type of government he formed in Libya. Jamahiriya refers to a country that belongs in all ways to its people.

nationalism: a political ideology that stresses strong feelings of loyalty to one's home or place of residence

Revolutionary Command Council (RCC): a twelve-member group formed by Qaddafi to organize a new government. Its members were all involved in the 1969 coup. The council was dissolved in 1977.

sanctions: restrictions imposed by a foreign government on another country's exports and imports to influence that country's government

Sharia: Islamic holy law, based on the Quran and on the rulings of Muslim scholars

Socialism: a political philosophy that stresses the economic equality of all citizens. Businesses and services are owned by the government so that all citizens may share equally in them.

sub-Saharan: African countries, including Sudan, Nigeria, and Ghana, that are located south of the Sahara

SOURCE NOTES

8 Barbara Slavin, e-mail message to author, February 2, 2007.

8 Craig S. Smith, "Qaddafi's Modern-Sounding Son Is a Riddle to the West," *New York Times*, December 14, 2004. Copyright 2004 by the New York Times Co. Reprinted with permission.

8 Debra A. Miller, *Modern Nations of the World—Libya*, (Farmington Hills, MI: Thomson Gale, 2005), 49. Reprinted with permission of Gale, a division of Thomson Learning.

17 Helen Chapin Metz, ed., *Libya: A Country Study*, 4th ed. (Washington, DC: Federal Research Division, Library of Congress, 1989), 35.

17 "Annex XI," *Treaty of Peace with Italy*, February 10, 1947, http://www.istrianet.org/istria/history/1800-present/ww2/1947_treaty-italy.htm (May 20, 2008).

27 Muammar al-Qaddafi, quoted in Corinne J. Naden and Rose Blue, *Heroes &*

Villains—Muammar al-Qaddafi, (Farmington Hills, MI: Thomson Gale, 2005), 22. Reprinted with permission of Gale, a division of Thomson Learning.

28 Ibid., 23.

36 Mohamed Eljahmi, "Qadhafi Unrepentant: Libya and the U.S." *Middle East Quarterly,* Winter 2006, 12–13.

37 Karl Marx and Friedrich Engels, *The Communist Manifesto and Other Revolutionary Writings,* Bob Blaisdell, ed. (Mineola, NY: Dover, 2003), 150.

40 Muammar Gaddafi, *The Green Book: The Social Basis of the Third Universal Law*, 1978, trans. Public Establishment for Publishing, Advertising and Distribution (Tripoli, Libya, 1978), 8.

52 Eljahmi, p. 18.

56 David Wallechinsky, "*PARADE's* Annual List of the World's 10 Worst Dictators," *PARADE*, January 22, 2006, http://www.parade.com/articles/editions/

2006/edition_01-22-2006/
Dictators (May 18, 2008).
Copyright David Wallechinsky.
Initially published in Parade
magazine. All rights reserved.

58 Eljahmi, 15.

67 Muammar Gaddafi, *The Green
Book: The Social Basis*, 35.

67 Ibid., 30.

69 Gaddafi, *The Green Book: The
Social Basis,* 48.

76 Muammar al-Qaddafi, quoted
in William A. Rugh, *Arab
Mass Media: Newspapers,
Radio, and Television in
Arab Politics* (Westport, CT:
Praeger Publishers, 2004), 188.
Reproduced with permission of
Greenwood Publishing Group,
Westport, CT.

76 Muammar Gaddafi, *The Green
Book: The Solution of the
Problem of Democracy*, 1973,
trans. Public Establishment for
Publishing, Advertising and
Distribution (Tripoli, Libya,
1978), 30.

87 Ibid., 13.

87 Muammar Qaddafi, *The Green
Book: Solution of the Economic
Problem: Socialism*, trans. Public
Establishment for Publishing,
Advertising and Distribution
(Tripoli, Libya, 1977), 17.

88 Muammar Qaddafi, *The Green
Book: The Social Basis,* 8.

89 Ibid., 47–48.

95 Muammar al-Qaddafi, quoted
in Naden and Blue, 63.

102 Foreign Broadcast Information
Service, "Al-Talhi Cited on
Ties with U.S." January 5, 1989,
15, quoted in Ronald Bruce
St. John, *Libya and the United
States: Two Centuries of Strife*
(Philadelphia: University of
Pennsylvania Press, 2002), 159.

104 Ibid., 14.

105 Ronald Reagan, " Promoting
Democracy and Peace" Speech
to British Parliament, June 8,
1982, The National Endowment
for Democracy (Washington,
D.C.) http://www.ned.org/
about/reagan-060882.html
(May 19, 2008).

110 John T. Rourke, *International
Politics on the World Stage*
(New York: McGraw-Hill, 2007),
405. Reprinted with permission
from McGraw-Hill Companies.

111 Muammar Qaddafi,
"Q:Qaddafi," January 1,
2002, *Military Quotes,* http://
www.military-quotes.com/
database/q.htm (May 19,
2008).

114 Elisabeth Rosenthal,
"HIV Injustice in Libya—
Scapegoating Foreign Medical
Professionals," *New England
Journal of Medicine,* December
14, 2006, 2,505–2,508.

116 Craig S. Smith and Matthew
Brunwasser, "Libya Again
Sentences Nurses and Doctor
to Die in H.I.V. Case," *New York
Times*, December 20, 2006.
Copyright 2006 by the New
York Times Co. Reprinted with
permission.

119 Mona el-Naggar, "Libya
Gingerly Begins Seeking
Economic but Not Political
Reform" *New York Times* March
2, 2007, http://www.nytimes.
com/2007/03/02/world/
africa/02libya.html?ex=13305
78000&en=c065f037b5ca5edc
&ei=5124&partner=permalink
&exprod=permalink (MAY 19,
2008).

120 "Libya: Release Gravely Ill
Political Prisoner" Human
Rights Watch, January 30,
2008, Http://hrw.org/english/
docs/2008/01/30/libya17927.
htm (May 12 2008).

125 Smith, "Qaddafi's Modern-
Sounding Son Is a Riddle to the
West."

126 "Gaddafi son unveils reform
plan" *BBC,* August 21, 2007,
http://news.bbc.co.uk/go/pr/
fr/-/2/hi/africa/6956351.stm
(May 19, 2008).

126 Smith, "Qaddafi's Modern-
Sounding Son Is a Riddle to the
West."

SELECTED BIBLIOGRAPHY

Arnold, Guy. "Libya: Foreign Policy under Qaddafi." In *Encyclopedia of African History*, vol. 2, edited by Kevin Shillington, 837–838. New York: Fitzroy Dearborn, 2005.

Baradent, Leon P. *Political Ideologies: Their Origins and Impact*. 9th ed. Saddle River, NJ: Pearson Prentice Hall, 2006.

Drake, Christine. "Morocco, Tunisia, and Libya: Diversity Within Unity." *Focus on Geography,* Winter 2006, 1–9.

Eljahmi, Mohamed. "Qadhafi Unrepentant: Libya and the U.S." *Middle East Quarterly,* Winter 2006, 11–20.

Harris, Lillian Craig. *Libya: Quadhafi's Revolution and the Modern State*. Boulder, CO: Westview Press, 1986.

Human Rights Watch. *World Report 2007*. January 15, 1007. http://hrw.org/englishwr2k7/docs/2007/01/11/libya14712.htm (May 18, 2008).

Magstadt, Thomas M. *Nations and Governments: Comparative Politics in Regional Perspective*. Belmont, CA: Wadsworth/Thomson Learning, 2005.

Metz, Helen Chapin, ed. *Libya: A Country Study*. 4th ed. Washington, DC: Federal Research Division, Library of Congress, 1989.

Miller, Debra A. *Modern Nations of the World—Libya*. Farmington Hills, MI: Thomson Gale, 2005.

Naden, Corinne J., and Rose Blue. *Heroes & Villains—Muammar al-Qaddafi*. Farmington Hills, MI: Thomson Gale, 2005.

Rosenthal, Elisabeth. "HIV Injustice in Libya—Scapegoating Foreign Medical Professionals." *New England Journal of Medicine,* December 14, 2006, 2,505–2,508.

Rourke, John T. *International Politics on the World Stage*. New York: McGraw-Hill, 2007.

Rugh, William A. *Arab Mass Media: Newspapers, Radio, and Television in Arab Politics.* Westport, CT: Praeger Publishers, 2004.

Simons, Geoff. *Libya: The Struggle for Survival.* New York: St. Martin's, 1993.

St. John, Ronald Bruce. *Libya and the United States: Two Centuries of Strife.* Philadelphia: University of Pennsylvania Press, 2002.

Stone, Richard. "To the Shores of Tripoli." *Science,* July 21, 2006, 285.

Vandewalle, Dirk. *A History of Modern Libya.* New York: Cambridge University Press, 2006.

Wallechinsky, David. "Who is the World's Worst Dictator?" *PARADE,* February 11, 2007. http://www.parade.com/articles/editions/2007/edition_02-11-2007/Dictators (May 19, 2008).

———. "Who Is the World's Worst Dictator?" *PARADE,* February 11, 2007, 6–8.

Wright, John. "Libya: Gaddafi (Qadhdhafi) and Jamahiriyya (Libyan Revolution)." In *Encyclopedia of African History,* vol. 2, edited by Kevin Shillington, 835–836. New York: Fitzroy Dearborn, 2005.

———. "Libya: Oil, Politics, and OPEC." In *Encyclopedia of African History,* vol. 2, edited by Kevin Shillington, 837–838. New York: Fitzroy Dearborn, 2005.

FURTHER READING AND WEBSITES

BOOKS

Baradent, Leon P. *Political Ideologies: Their Origins and Impact.* 9th ed. Saddle River, NJ: Pearson Prentice Hall, 2006. This book examines differences and similarities of a variety of political philosophies from around the world, including capitalism, Socialism, and Communism.

Di Piazza, Francesca. *Libya in Pictures.* Minneapolis: Twenty-First Century Books, 2006. This book offers information and photos about modern life in Libya, as well as the nation's history and resources.

Goldstein, Margaret J. *Israel in Pictures.* Minneapolis: Twenty-First Century Books, 2004. This book unravels the history of Israel and describes its government, economy, people, geography, and cultural life.

Gottfried, Ted. *Libya: Desert Land in Conflict.* Brookfield, CT: Millbrook Press, 1994. This book for young adults presents the powerful forces that shaped modern Libya and Qaddafi's controversial rule through the early 1990s.

Headlam, George. *Yasser Arafat.* Minneapolis: Twenty-First Century Books, 2004. A friend of Muammar al-Qaddafi, Yasser Arafat has been a key figure in the Palestinian-Israeli conflict for more than thirty years. This biography describes his rise to power as founder of the Palestinian National Liberation Movement (Fatah) and later as a speaker against terrorism.

Miller, Debra A. *Modern Nations of the World—Libya.* Farmington Hills, MI: Thomson Gale, 2005. This book offers a great deal of background about Libya, its culture, and government. It provides current information about Qaddafi and the country's prospects for the future.

WEBSITES

Amnesty International

http://web.amnesty.org/library/Index/ENGMDE190022004

This is a link to the April 27, 2004, Amnesty International report on Libya's human rights violations, called *Libya: Time to Make Human Rights a Reality.*

The Green Book

http://www.geocities.com/athens/8744/zgbover.htm

This is a link to the full English-language text of Colonel Qaddafi's *The Green Book*, in which he describes his political philosophy.

Human Rights Watch World Report 2007: Libya

http://hrw.org/englishwr2k7/docs/2007/01/11/libya14712.htm

Human Rights Watch offers yearly reports on the human rights records of countries around the world. It includes their policies on matters such as political prisoners and the death penalty. This link is to the 2007 report on Libya, but a vast collection of other data is also available at http://hrw.org.

Muammar Al Gathafi Official Site

http://www.algathafi.org/html-english/index.htm

This English-language site offers speeches and comments from Muammar Qaddafi on a variety of topics.

The National Conference of the Libyan Opposition

http://libya-nclo.org/English%20Page.htm

This is the English-language version of a website dedicated to the removal of Qaddafi and the establishment of a democracy in Libya.

Visual Geography Series: Libya

http://www.vgsbooks.com

Visit vgsbooks.com, the home page of the Visual Geography Series®, and click on Libya for all sorts of useful online information. Link to geographical, historical, demographic, cultural, and economic websites. The vgsbooks.com site is a great resource for late-breaking news and statistics.

INDEX

PHOTO ACKNOWLEDGMENTS

AUTHOR BIOGRAPHY

Kimberly L. Sullivan holds a Ph.D in political science and has been a college instructor for more than ten years. In addition to writing nonfiction, she also writes fiction for young adult readers. A lifelong Illinois resident, she lives in the Chicago suburbs with her husband and son.